Review of *Homeless: The Truth?*

Homeless: The Truth? was such a magnificent read! I respect honesty, and an earnest desire for truth. Couple that with love of beauty and love of our fellow human beings, as one finds in Tricia. One cannot help but embrace her and root for her as she stumbles from one agonizing decision or consequence to another, and cheer for her as she grows in courage and understanding, and gradually Grace! Beyond the draw of the story itself is the budding enlightenment that I feel within *me*, as I recognize some things, or understand other things, alongside Tricia. I am eagerly looking forward to the third volume of this series!

— Marina Holland

HOMELESS:
THE TRUTH?

Magdalen Dugan

I said to my soul, be still, and wait without hope
For hope would be hope for the wrong thing; wait without love
For love would be love of the wrong thing; there is yet faith
But the faith and the love and the hope are all in the waiting.

– T.S. Eliot, "East Coker," The Four Quartets

"It was a long time ago, and I've let it go, except when a name or a face or the piercing realization of how wrong we were returns to haunt me. If I'm a different person now, and I am, the ones I remember must also have changed, but that doesn't mean we should simply forget. We have to tell the story so that maybe people won't make the same mistakes. But don't tell it as if it were just my story. It's so many stories, so many perspectives wound together like the maze we walked."

– Tricia Riley Rostov, Professor, Author,
and Orthodox Christian

TABLE OF CONTENTS

PART ONE

IF I KNEW THE WAY

Two Roads

Tricia Riley, February 1975

"Open your eyes, Tricia," Jana said.

"They're wide open. Just listen to me. I have two choices, two roads I could follow –"

"Oh no, not the Frost poem again –"

"Give me a break, Jana. I'm not discussing poetry – this is my life I'm talking about."

Jana shrugged and lit a cigarette. A Kool, the brand she chain-smoked. Tricia smoked less, mainly while writing, but then it was Lucky Strikes with no filter. Tricia thought her choice was significant, but Jana said Tricia thought every little detail of her own life was significant, as if she were a character in a novel.

That night Tricia was sure she actually did see a road extending to her left and to her right, disappearing into the distance on either side – two possible lives on alternate timelines – although it may have been in her mind's eye because she wasn't high that night and she wasn't worthy of a vision. Maybe the road she remembered ever after was only Telegraph Avenue, extending north and south from the corner of 62nd Street, where she was sitting on a stone wall whose cold dampness seeped through the seat of her jeans.

Beside her on that stone cold sober wall sat Jana, her best friend and nemesis, who'd just gotten her special education credential at Buffalo State and moved across the country to Santa Cruz with her boyfriend, Chad. Jana had taken the bus up to Berkeley that night to try to talk some sense into her unpragmatic and easily misled friend, and now she shifted her ever present cigarette to her left hand and dug the long fingers of her right into Tricia's arm.

"You need to use your brain this time, Tricia, not just your heart. You're about to throw away everything you've built here."

"Just listen for a minute," Tricia said. "Remember how before I moved out here I wanted to join up with artists, to create a better culture? You were behind that, weren't you?"

"So?"

"So I never found a group of artists to join up with exactly, but this is even better. In HOME people do want to transform the culture, but they're not just doing that. They want to grow as spiritual beings. They take vows, study, and learn to serve."

"Oh, yeah? Who do they 'serve?'"

"God, Jana. They serve God."

"Mmmhmm."

"And they said if I joined them I could still write, and eventually teach. Be a part of something greater than I am."

Jana rolled her eyes. "And you need their permission to do that? You've spent more than a year building your life here, Trica. You've got a place to live, a way to pay your rent, and people to share your poetry with. If you really want to teach, you can go back and finish that degree you abandoned at the eleventh hour without even giving it a chance. Now you want to give up everything again, to live like a fake nun with a bunch of losers who can't figure out whether they're Presbyterian or Rosicrucian. You say you'd never even consider becoming a Krishna or a Sufi because they aren't

Christians, but at least those religions have some history. These HOME phonies are making it up as they go."

"They're doing something radically different, and that's just the point. The Holy Order of Mystical Evangelists is striving to practice pure religion. Where have the organized religions gotten us so far? They've deteriorated into dead forms and hypocrisy. Do you know what Brother Jarrell said last night? The Catholic Church left me a long time before I left it."

"No argument there. But why would you trust these people any better? Is it just because they're as idealistic as you are? You're taking their word for an awful lot, Tricia. What are they basing their teachings on?"

Just then a bird hidden in the live oak above them mimicked the call and trill of a wood thrush, a bird Tricia listened for when she was hiking, but she knew it was a mockingbird and not a thrush. The song was too passionate and insistent, without context or restraint. That was the problem with mockingbirds – the songs weren't theirs – it was as if they had to force the music.

She needed to go somewhere, do something. She'd always felt that, and urgently. For a long time, it had been to travel to Europe – the history, the art, the beauty – to somehow make that part of herself. Then she had gone to Europe and had found something, yes, and had grown, yes, but had left disappointed. California had offered what seemed endless opportunity and freedom, but to what end?

"Free yourself, be yourself," one popular song promised. It sounded so simple, so beautiful, but it couldn't mean living as part of the counterculture to free her true self, because she'd been up to her eyeballs in the counterculture and that self wasn't free.

She'd once confided to a poetry professor, "If I could, I'd fly into the sun."

"You'd be burned to ashes," he answered.

"It wouldn't matter."

Maybe now she was slowly becoming more real. At the advice of the Brothers, she hadn't gotten high for more than a month, and for longer than that she hadn't gotten into a relationship with a guy just to prove she was okay the way she'd been doing ever since she'd lost Jonathan and a part of herself.

She could think clearly enough now to see those two roads – maybe not even a right and a wrong, but clearly a right and a left. She could keep living the way she had been for the last year – writing poetry, doing readings at Moe's and The Café Mediterraneum, practicing yoga, collecting unemployment checks and men – the path of least resistance that just about everybody around her was taking. Of course writing poetry was contributing something to the world, but she had to admit even then that less of her life was spent actually writing than living some notion she had of being a poet. Of course, that could change. She could get better at her craft, publish, even finish her degree and teach. She could clean up that act, that path, but she would still be the self that wasn't free.

Or she could join the Brotherhood – The Holy Order of Mystical Evangelists. They promised that she would be part of transforming the cultural and spiritual mess nearly everyone was in, and ushering in a new, more enlightened age. It had been revealed by God to their founder, Father Peter, that the chosen ones of HOME would be His servants in renewing the world. They said Tricia was called to be one of them, that it was her calling that led her to them. This was her chance to be part of something that really mattered, and to actually change into someone better.

"I wake up every day afraid of dying before I can figure out how to live,' she had told Brother Jarrell just a few weeks ago, surprised that she was actually confiding this to another person.

"Yes," he answered, "I know what you mean. It's a good start to realize you feel that way. Become Illumined and you'll find a way to deal with life and death, and stop waking up every morning afraid."

If that alone were true….

But how could she explain all this to Jana, who used to know her better than anybody – what she wanted and what she feared, her strengths and her weaknesses – and who now couldn't hear her at all. Tricia wished her friend had been there at the Brother House through the hours of Bible study that opened up a new way of life. Those classes had shown Tricia how the truth is one, but human beings mess it up with what the Brothers called "religiosity." Father Peter had received messages from God and had written and published them in *The Book of Revelation*. The life-vowed Brothers and Sisters were allowed to read them all. These Brothers, who understood so much, surely must be telling the truth.

"Tricia? Tricia! I asked you what they're basing their teachings on. Surely you've thought about that."

"Oh. The Bible, to start with."

"Then why, for God's sake, don't you just go to a Christian church? You never stopped believing."

"No, I never stopped believing in Christ, but I stopped believing in churches, at least any of the churches I know about. And HOME is different."

"Yeah, really different."

"They're connecting the truth across all the great religions. Remember what I was studying before I left State?"

"Yes I do, and I remember that you had a breakdown while you were so-called studying."

Tricia breathed, sighed. "Okay. But that was almost two years ago. This is different, and I'm different. And you have to know how much good these people do, working with alcoholics and drug addicts, feeding them, teaching them."

"Brainwashing them, harvesting them. How many of those 'Brothers and Sisters' were drunks and druggies that HOME 'helped', Tricia? And now they're 'the chosen ones' who work day and night to turn over their paychecks to this supposedly 'holy' order."

"They're forgiven, Jana, and they're practicing the vow of poverty by holding all things in common. Didn't Jesus preach to the prostitutes and tax collectors, and make them disciples?"

"Don't ask me. Jesus is your thing, not mine. But if you're going to be a Jesus freak, why don't you just do that, like Jonathan and Susanne? There must be a Campus Crusade for Christ at Berkeley. At least those people are trying to be honest and even if they brainwash you, they let you out six days a week to have some kind of normal life."

"That isn't what you said when Jonathan told us he'd been 'saved'. You said how could somebody who's seen as much as Jonathan put the blinders back on."

"Yeah, well, it's relative," Jana said. "He put on blinders. You're putting a freaking bag over your head so you can hide from the world. Sure it's scary here in the real world, Tricia, not knowing what's going to happen from one day to the next, let alone for all eternity. But admitting that has some integrity, a lot more than living in a fairy tale."

There's a lot of truth in fairy tales, Tricia wanted to say, but stopped herself. Jana wouldn't be able to hear it. Fairy tales have more substance than most of the daily news, she argued silently, and certainly more than most of the classes at Buffalo State where professors and students laughed at faith but had no alternatives other than escaping into drinking, sex, and power. Those couldn't be the answers. Fairy tales are about universal problems and suffering, and about overcoming them. Now against her will, against her judgement, she was crying. Jana jumped down from the wall. Tricia opened her arms for a hug, but Jana grabbed her shoulders and shook her.

"Tricia, you're not okay. Let me find you a therapist up here. You can probably get one for free since you make about twenty dollars a week or something, and if not I can help out." Jana was starting a "real" job teaching special ed at a junior high in the fall, and would be making some "real" money.

"I'm fine," Tricia said, catching her breath. "And you're right – it *is* a fairy tale, with a journey and a fork in the road. It *is* the Frost poem – it's a prototype. Don't you get it?"

Jana looked at her fiercely, her right eyebrow arched high. "I quote, 'I'm not discussing poetry – this is my life I'm talking about.'"

Berkeley, February 1975. Stars in the cold, clear sky mirrored the brilliant shards of the city's million fragile hearts. Was there anyone who wasn't suffering?

"Don't worry, Jana. Whatever I decide, I'll still be on the ragged edge, still scared every day when I wake up – maybe not so much of dying now as of living – if that's how you define having integrity."

In fact, Tricia had already chosen, and that choice eliminated a world of other possibilities. Maybe she sensed that even then, and was just waiting for some kind of confirmation. Maybe that night Jana, with more love and skepticism than most parents, provided the confirmation she needed, simply by refusing to understand.

CHAPTER TWO

SCAPEGOAT

Timmy Riley, April 1975

"She wants to join a cult," Mrs. Riley said, clenching her hand around Tricia's letter, tears in her eyes.

"Ah, Mom, it can't really be a cult. Tricia's kind of crazy, but not that crazy. Who'd purposely join a cult and let wierdos control their life?" Timmy said.

"It is a cult, Timmy. She is a Catholic girl who wants to belong to a group started by a lapsed Catholic who got himself ordained somewhere, maybe the Episcopalians, and became a Rosicrucian, and now claims he's had visions and revelations about the New Age."

"How do you know that, Mom?"

"I talked to the Bishop. He knows."

She had to be exaggerating. She was obviously really upset, and it was going to be hard to tell what was going on until he read the letter for himself. Mom was so loving and committed to her family, but out of touch with the world, emotional, and kind of gullible. On the other hand, Dad was so closed-minded he hadn't let Tricia join the Girl Scouts because the meetings were held in the Presbyterian church and her Catholic mind might be polluted. Tricia herself hadn't communicated with Timmy much for the past two years since she left school again and moved to California to write and find herself or whatever.

"If she would just go to Mass and talk to a priest she could get straightened out," Mrs. Riley said. "She hasn't been to church for a very long time."

Mom and Dad were super-Catholic in the old-fashioned way – priests and nuns were always right, the Pope was infallible, there was only one way to get to heaven. Timmy was Catholic too – he always had been and he didn't see any reason not to be – but he also believed in being open-minded. People worship God in a lot of ways, and who was he to judge? His girlfriend, Caroline, wasn't Catholic but she believed in God and Jesus, and she was kind to everybody (not to mention really pretty) and that was good enough for him. Maybe Tricia's holy order of whatever wasn't wrong, just different. He couldn't imagine that Tricia – intensely spiritual Tricia – had stopped believing in God and Jesus. But she really hated the Vatican II changes. She said the Catholic Church had thrown away its beauty and abandoned its people, that God can't be worshipped in that ugliness. Beauty will save the world, she said – it was something from a Russian writer she liked a lot.

Besides, Tricia had always been different. Okay, Dad had always been different, even strange, even sociopathic. And violent, but not toward Timmy. Tricia usually got the worst of it, except maybe for Mom, but Mom just took it and took it. Tricia was the one who stood up to Dad, so he yelled at her the worst and hit her a lot. One time he took a broom and beat her down the cellar stairs. She had a lot of bruises and a cut on her leg and her cheek from falling, but she never cried, only looked at everybody with a kind of fire in her eyes. Afterwards she said it'd be worth it if he'd break her arm or something so she could go to the hospital and people would find out about Dad, pillar of the Church, upstanding member of the community. But he never broke anything. Except maybe Mom's heart. Maybe he broke Tricia's heart too for a while there, but for a long time now she'd been way more mad than sad.

For sure Dad never broke her spirit. She was like a wild horse penned up in a little corral and not exercised. She wouldn't do what Dad wanted, like get good grades in high school, even though the teachers said she had a high I.Q., and she read books like crazy, hundreds of them, just never the ones she was supposed to read. She lashed out and bit people with her words sometimes, even people who cared about her, until she finally broke down the fence and ran away when she was eighteen.

Dad was nicer to Timmy, his only son. They cut the grass together or shoveled the snow, and sometimes Dad took him to the high school where he taught, to help clean the blackboard and count the English textbooks before putting them away for the summer. Sometimes he played checkers with Timmy, and sometimes Timmy would sit on the chair next to the couch where Dad would stretch out after work, and watch "cowboy shows" with him while he ate his supper and relaxed enough to fall asleep. Dad loved those cowboy shows, and Timmy guessed he must have liked them too because now he was planning to go west to Colorado with Caroline, where the mountains are close, the skies are clear blue, and you can drive for miles without seeing another living person. They had decided they wouldn't want to live anywhere else.

Timmy had been sixteen when Tricia left home. The conversation went something like this:

Tricia: "Dad, I need to talk with you about something important."

Dad: "Make it quick. The next show's going to start in a couple minutes.

Tricia: "I got really good grades at the community college this year, so I applied to Syracuse University for journalism, and I got in! I got a grant for the tuition, and a Work Study job for expenses. I just need help with the dorm fee. I want this really, really badly, Dad, and you said you'd help out if I got good grades. Will you help me?"

Dad: "Journalism? Girls don't become journalists. You can be a teacher or a nurse like your friends are doing. If you go to a teacher's college, I'll help with your living expenses."

Tricia: "Dad, women <u>do</u> become journalists. Some of the professors in the Journalism Department at Syracuse are women, and some of the writers on *The Buffalo Evening News* staff are women, and some of the journalists covering the Vietnam War are women. Everybody says I'm a good writer. I can do this."

Dad: "Over my dead body. You have no business going all the way to Syracuse when you can live at home and go to school in Buffalo and become a teacher. That's the end of it."

Tricia: "But Dad –"

Dad (yelling): "I SAID, that's the end of it!" He turned the T.V. back on.

Tricia did cry that night, but it was definitely because she was so mad. She charged to the back of the house, where Mom, Rita, Brigit and Timmy followed her like they always did after a blow-up. They shut her bedroom door and she yelled and cried and cried and yelled, while the cowboy show started and the sound of western music and gunfire in the living room masked her shouts. Mom tried to calm her down, Rita and Brigit looked on in sympathy, and Timmy studied her process.

She said she was leaving as soon as possible. She said Dad hadn't really surprised her, and she had a backup plan. She was giving notice at the supermarket tomorrow. She was taking all her savings and going to Europe with her classmate from school, to backpack and to write. Then maybe she'd go to school in Australia where she could earn free tuition if she stayed there and worked, and she would never come back again. She said she was leaving in less than a month, like the scapegoat in the Bible, with the whole family's sins on her back. Timmy didn't have a clue what she was talking about, but a lot of times he didn't. Like when she went storming away from the outdoor Mass at Bishop Ignatius where Timmy went to high school. It was the Consecration and they were playing "Purple Haze." He followed her down the street.

"Now what, Tricia?"

"How can they play that song at the Consecration? Are they insane? No, wait – rhetorical question. They ARE insane. What's next, nuns with tambourines dancing during the Mass?"

"But you like Jimi Hendrix. We've listened to 'Purple Haze' together a hundred times –"

"Yeah, Timmy, we have, and he's great – in your room. Not in church. Not while they're quoting Jesus giving us His Body and Blood."

Timmy didn't get it, but Tricia was positive. She probably never went back to a Catholic church after that. That was Tricia. What she believed in, she did, and nothing could stop her. She was going to break down that fence and run free.

And Timmy knew that night, one of the last nights that Tricia slept at home, that breaking down that fence was what he needed to do, too. He knew it might take a couple of years to get the money together, but he was leaving. He was going to the supermarket the next day, right after she did, to apply for her job.

That is exactly what he'd done. He'd started out as a grocery clerk like Tricia had been, and worked his way up to assistant manager. The beauty of that supermarket was that it was walking distance from their house, because of course he didn't have a car yet. Now he'd saved most of the money he needed to start his own life, and found a pretty and kind travelling companion too. He could understand almost everything Tricia had done up until now, and the next time he saw her he'd thank her for being the first to break free.

But joining a cult? He was going to get a hold of that letter and figure things out for himself.

CHAPTER THREE

The Beginning,
or One of the Beginnings

Tricia Riley, December 1, 1974

Tricia was just leaving the Café Mediterraneum clutching her poetry notebook when Brother Jarrell first approached her. Well over six feet tall, slim, and angular, in a full-length brown wool robe tied at the waist with a hemp cord, he looked more like an angel than a man. That suited her fine at the moment, because she was sick of men.

"Was there a reading tonight?" He nodded toward her notebook.

She shook her head. "I've just been writing."

"May I see?"

"It's not ready yet."

"Don't you have anything that's finished? I'd like to hear something."

She didn't have anything with her, but this was a rare request to share her poetry, so she recited from memory a short poem in which the speaker was both a woman and a river winding to the sea, and in neither case had much need for men. When she finished, he didn't praise the poem or ask questions about it, but simply thanked her. It was the right response – an authentic response, she thought – and it inclined her to keeping talking with him. They sat at an outdoor table in front of the café and talked for about an hour about poetry. He liked Eliot, too, and Shakespeare, and Williams, and Dickinson, not just Bob Dylan and Jerry Garcia, as awesome as they were. He'd read more classic poets than just about anybody she'd met in Berkeley. When she said so, he explained that he had been majoring in English literature at U.C., Berkeley when he met the Holy Order of Mystical Evangelists. He was so inspired by their message that he was compelled to drop out and join them. Tricia could relate, not only because she had dropped out of school twice, but because nearly everybody she knew in Berkeley had dropped out of something, be it school or a job or a relationship, to find themselves.

"Did you know that Scriptures are a kind of poetry?" he asked at last.

"Of course. I like to read the Psalms out loud, and the Gospel of John, and Isaiah –"

He widened his eyes so dramatically it made her laugh.

Evidently her jeans, long hair, and bare feet, combined with their Telegraph Avenue location, had led him to misjudge her.

"Yeah, I read the Bible," she said. "I'm not an atheist, not even an agnostic. I'm sure I believe – just not sure what I need to do about it. Does that make any sense?"

"Of course it does. You want to learn about God through Christ without being limited by organized religion. That's what we're doing in the Holy Order of Mystical Evangelists, Tricia."

To learn about God through Christ. Tricia believed in salvation through Jesus Christ. But it wasn't enough to know that God exists, or even to believe in Him and "accept Him as Savior" the way that Jonathan and his friends talked about. The question was, how was she supposed to live? The Christian churches all had answers to that, but after breaking from Catholicism she didn't trust any of them anymore. Maybe it wouldn't do any harm to check out these people. She attended a class at the Brother House the next Wednesday.

The first time she went with her housemate, Georgie, a woman in her forties who'd had a very hard life but wanted a better one. When Tricia told her about meeting Brother Jarrell, her eyes widened and she told Tricia about her visits to the Brothers, how kind they were, how much she had learned from them about God and herself. She said she'd be excited to bring a new inquirer. It seemed to mean so much to her that Tricia let her believe that it was she, and not Brother Jarrell, who had convinced her to attend.

*****

Brother Jarrell met them at the door that first night.

"So you've come. I'm so glad." He laughed nervously, and gave Tricia an awkward, one-armed hug before turning to her house mate. "Hello, Georgie. Good to see you again."

The house where the Brothers lived was a cottage in the Berkeley style – a large front porch, a small living room converted into a chapel, a very small, cozy dining room where classes were held, a spacious kitchen where the Brothers had set out plates of fruit and nuts. The rooms were cozy with lots of wood – hardwood floors and beams and fireplace lintel – and warm walls the color of cream. The furniture was second-hand, which fit with the popular value of voluntary simplicity, but comfortable enough.

Entering the dining room, Tricia learned that the speaker for the evening, seated in an armchair in a corner from which he could see everyone, was not Brother Jarrell, but the House Master, Father Todd, who stood to greet her. He proved to be a six foot two Texan who could use, or drop, a heavy drawl as it suited him. Like Brother Jarrell, he wore a Franciscan-style brown robe tied at the waist with a rope, and leather sandals; his hair was short, and he was clean-shaven. He gave the impression of sincerity and authority, sternness and kindness, like a good father.

The format of the class was surprisingly similar to those Tricia had attended in Catholic Church halls as a teen – a handful of people gathered to read Scripture and discuss how it applied to their lives. What was different was the focus, not how to live by church rules, but how to live so as not to die –the one question Tricia asked herself every morning when she woke up. They read from the Gospel of John – Christ's words to Martha, whose brother, Lazarus, had just died and was about to be raised from the dead: "He who lives and believes in me will never die. Do you believe this?" Tricia's heartbeat quickened.

Father Todd snapped the Bible closed with one hand and reached the other hand around the room in a circle toward his seated listeners, meeting their eyes one person at a time. "Do you believe this?" he repeated. "This is what the Master asks you."

Wait – who was the Master? Was this man saying he was the Master?

"Excuse me a second, please. Who is the Master? Is that you?" she asked.

Father Todd laughed a belly laugh. "Georgie, am I the Master?"

"No," Georgie giggled. "The Master is Jesus."

Tricia breathed again. "Okay, thanks."

"You're paying attention, though, Tricia. So maybe you want to answer the question. Do you believe this?"

Did she believe this? Somehow, in eighteen years of Catholic services and Catholic school classes, she had never truly heard this question, never asked it of herself. Surely it had been read in church. That night she heard it as a question that offered the answer to all her questions. And it was Jesus asking the question – Jesus. Of course it was, from the Gospel of John.

"Well, Jesus is God, and He said this, so it must be true. It's just – how? I know I'm supposed to have eternal life, but I don't think that happens by itself, and I don't know how to put the two things together, eternity and me. I mean, how am I supposed to connect with Jesus's words now, or with Jesus, in 1974, in freaking Berkeley, California where everybody's nuts including me?" She didn't quite finish the last part before she was sobbing and Brother Jarrell was getting up to put a hand on her shoulder.

Father Todd smiled slightly and nodded. "That's a good start. You have faith in God, which is good, but the Gospel says that even the demons believe and tremble, so no, that's not enough by itself. Let me ask you this, how do you know you're supposed to have eternal life?"

Nobody talked until Tricia stopped sobbing and blew her nose on the tissue Georgie handed her. She breathed for a minute before she got her voice, but something fueled her desire to talk. No one had ever asked her questions like this before, and they were questions about what was most important to her.

"I can just feel it inside myself – something big, limitless really. It mostly stays inside. Sometimes it comes out a little in poems or when I'm talking with someone I trust but there aren't too many I trust. The rest of the time I forget about it and just do stuff. The worst times are when I know it's there but I'm not paying attention to it. Like I'm apart from it. Like Yeats says about the heart, 'sick with desire and fastened to a dying animal, it knows not what it is.'"

"Whoa, heavy," said Georgie.

"Yeah, it's like that for me, too," said a bearded man sitting across from her. "It's a kind of place inside – big and free. I've only been there a couple of times, mostly when I was camping in Washington State on Mount Rainier. Later, I kept dropping acid to try to get back into it, but it wasn't the same. People say LSD makes you free but it doesn't work that way. It can do other stuff, I guess, but not that."

"No, no, wait," said another man sitting next to him. "I've had visions on LSD."

"Those are called hallucinations, not visions," Father Todd said, "and you'll want to know the difference between the two. Tricia, I want to ask you another question. You say you believe in the Master, but what else does He say you need to do?"

"Live and believe. He who lives and believes in Me will never die. I believe. I don't know how to live."

"That's what we want to teach you."

Maybe a way. A path.

The rest of that evening they discussed responses to Christ's question, but not only in the Gospels. Father Todd quoted from the Torah, the Zoroastrian Avesta, and the Tao Te Ching – all talking about a way to live forever. This openness to the truth wherever it might be found resonated with Tricia's earlier realization, while she was discovering the similarities in the beliefs of many ancient people. Those studies had not weakened her faith as her professor suggested, but strengthened it. God had been revealing Himself to every culture through history, preparing them to receive Jesus; some people had been shown more, or understood more, and some less. Not just the Jews, but some ancient Egyptians and Babylonians and Native Americans had believed in one God, and called Him Aten, or Ahura Mazda, or Wakan Tanka. What she had glimpsed wasn't the simplistic idea that all religions were the same or even equivalent – not at all! Some religions worshipped someone or something other than God, even demons like Paul says in the Epistles. It was simply that God was showing Himself to everyone who wanted to know, that He was a lot bigger than the opinions of one group of people, that if people would seek Him, they could find Him.

She would seek Him. She was going to keep attending these classes.

CHAPTER FOUR

A Lady of the Canyon

Brother Jarrell, December 22, 1974

Brother Jarrell was afraid this new girl he'd recruited might be trouble. Not trouble of the drug addiction variety or the angry at God variety, but something else more complicated. After many meetings, he still couldn't figure her out. Looking back through his journal, he found conflicting impressions.

Sunday, December 1

At first glance Tricia could have been any drugged out hippie leaving the Café Mediterraneum to walk barefoot down Telegraph Avenue – early twenties, hair to her knees, ripped jeans, and a dazed look in her eyes. But she was cleaner than most, better dressed, and carrying a notebook. After speaking with her I decided the dazed look was from writing and dreaming, not drugs.

It wasn't hard to get her involved in conversation once I mentioned poetry. The original poem she recited for me was not bad in a romantic, self-focused kind of way, but the poets she talked about were the real thing, ones who ask the big life questions and point to answers. And then she said she read the Bible. So much for appearances.

December 4, 1974

The new recruit, Tricia, came to class tonight. It's obvious that she wants answers, and she appears to sincerely want something more, but she's been living a very worldly life, which tells me she doesn't know herself well. Something she said tonight floored me, though – that she feels separated from who she really is. Unless she has a mental condition, that's probably a sign that her spiritual cleansing has started and, if she isn't already beginning to be illumined, she is at least ready to start the journey. She admitted to doing a lot of drugs before she came to California, which is ironic, because when she arrived in drugged-out Berkeley, she pretty much stopped, except for smoking dope now and then. She said that before, in Buffalo, she was trying to lose herself, but here she's been trying to find herself. That's also a hopeful sign.

December 11, 1974

What concerns me about Tricia is her intensity, almost a desperation, as if she has to find answers and find them right away. The Path takes time and patience. It will no doubt be very difficult for her to learn patience. And she is scrappy, again tonight asking Father Todd pointed questions during class and ready to argue. He usually responds with wry humor, as if she were a little girl with a big imagination, and maybe she is, but how will the vow of obedience sit with someone like her? Willful as she is, though, she isn't really independent because she's always looking for affirmation, for love. Evidently she's had a lot of boyfriends, but never for long. She will need to focus on her discipleship without looking to other people to validate her. She's already attached to me but that's just what happens with young women and the Brothers. I'll have to be very careful with her emotions until she takes her vows. In time, she'll realize that it's the life, not me, that's attracting her.

December 18, 1974

Tricia is still coming to class, and I think she will enter training. Hopefully, her time as a novice and a student will teach her the difference between art and life. I love art too, and beauty of every kind, maybe as much as she does, but it seems to intoxicate her. She sees herself as a character in a story or a song – not very balanced. I've tried to laugh it off, but she doesn't stop. The latest was Joni Mitchell's "Ladies of the Canyon," only she changed the name from Trina to Tricia:

> Tricia wears her wampum beads
> She fills her drawing book with lines….
> Vine and leaf are filigreed
> And her coat's a second-hand one
> Trimmed in antique luxury….

In a psychology class at CAL, I learned that when people talk about themselves in the third person it's a sign of an unhealthy mind. Something to talk with Father Todd about.

CHAPTER FIVE

O HOLY NIGHT

Tricia Riley, December 24, 1974

It was Christmas Eve, and the weather was finally starting to feel a little like winter. The sun was warm most of the day, but towards sunset the air went cool and then cold, and the sky went from deep blue to black, with thousands of stars that were appropriately cold and hopeful.

Tricia knew that this wasn't just any night. It wasn't a matter of dogma, which she had rejected, or habit, because she and Jana had sworn to themselves and each other to be self-examined and authentic, and they had scrutinized their assumptions. Tricia's belief was a matter of experience. She had encountered the person this night was about, not in visions but in her heart. She knew this person was real, and good, and wanted good for her. She just hadn't figured out yet what to do about that.

The year before, her first Christmas in Berkeley, she'd set a standard for failure. That morning last year she'd sat on the porch awhile doing what she knew how to do – breathing and looking at the sky. That was fine, but she knew it wasn't enough. She read the Gospel about the birth of Jesus, and that was better. But then Jana and Chad arrived from Santa Cruz. She was glad to see her friends, but this was an entirely different occasion for them than it was for her because when they'd left the Catholic church they'd decided to be humanists. They basically believed in being interesting and ethical people, in doing things they thought were good, but not in anything higher than themselves. At the same time, they indeed were interesting and ethical people, and they were the closest thing she had to a family. No excuses, though. It was Christmas and she had agreed to just have a party. It was her own stupid fault.

Chad brought a game of RISK (world domination, anyone?) Tricia contributed a bottle of Southern Comfort. (She didn't remember providing anything to eat all day – likely she didn't. She did remember that they killed the bottle, and ever afterward she couldn't smell Southern Comfort without her stomach retching.) Jana, true to character, brought *Cat's Cradle,* arguably Vonnegut's most blasphemous, iconoclastic novel. So there they were – not three wise kings but three foolish beggars with gifts borrowed from the world, the flesh, and the devil.   They took their accustomed positions, seated cross-legged on the floor of Tricia's second story bedroom. Sun streamed through the windows in the December afternoon.

"How do you like this place?" Tricia asked. "Would you say it's an improvement on the apartment over the junk store back in Allentown?"

Jana laughed sarcastically. "You mean no rats, no mold, no blizzards?"

"Do you ever hear anything from Gabriel?" Tricia asked.

Jana shook her head. "Good riddance. The best thing about being with him was breaking up and finding Chad." She rested her long-fingered, silver-decked hand on her boyfriend's knee. "I did get a postcard from Jonathan and Susanne. They set a wedding date in June."

Tricia didn't answer. The pain was still there, but she could be happy for them. Jonathan had found a less complicated woman than Tricia, which was what he wanted, as well as joining the Campus Crusade for Christ – a simple creed for a complex man, but one that seemed to speak to him. And Tricia had long since stopped hoping to be with him.

They started their festivities with the novel, Jana reading aloud in her rich alto voice while Chad and Tricia sipped whiskey and soaked in the sun pouring through the open windows. Ah, California. How could this be winter?

Tricia liked the story well enough at the beginning – interesting characters, a tense end-of-the-world plot that resonated with the way they were all feeling about their upside-down world. But Jana had introduced it as a profound statement about the human condition, so Tricia knew they were headed for Jana's chosen land of absurdity and pointlessness. Sure enough, by the final pages the author had neatly deprived the reader of hope, even of any point in living.

Jana closed the book with her sideways smirk of a smile. Tricia was determined not to get into it with Jana again, so she said nothing, even though it was Christmas Day, and even though there was too a point in living.

They agreed to play a game of RISK in which, after many hours, Tricia succeeded in defending Irkutsk and achieving world domination, and during which they finished the bottle of Southern Comfort.

But what had the day been? When Chad and Jana fell asleep that night, Tricia sat for a long time on the front porch, thinking how moving across the country had not brought her closer to becoming a better person as she had hoped it would. She had to admit that she wasn't living the way she believed, but she didn't know where to find a framework to live better.

Now, a year later on Christmas Eve, she had a chance to observe this night somewhat the way she believed – not exactly in a church, but in a place very much like a church, where she could at least sense the expansiveness of her own being and recognize its relation to the great Being. At the Brother House, other people would know it was a holy night two thousand years ago, and a holy night again now. She imagined candles lighted in the living room chapel, maybe poinsettias or a vase of roses, people meditating quietly, reading Scripture, singing together, and sharing something to eat and drink. This was the kind of Christmas Eve she'd been wanting for a long time.

She walked down Telegraph Avenue through the deliciously brisk air and tilted her head to look at the stars, always brighter at this time of year. She was carrying a zucchini and rice casserole to share, and in the bag on her shoulder she carried another gift – the collected poems of T.S. Eliot that Jana had given her, knowing how strongly he spoke to her. This wasn't Scripture, but poetry that resonated with Scripture.

What we call the beginning is often the end
And to make an end is to make a beginning.
The end is where we start from....

She would share these hopeful words tonight, on this holy night, when the stars really were brightly shining, and she did not have to be convinced of joy. But as she was about to turn the corner from Telegraph onto a side street, she saw him.

He was probably only one of many homeless people on the street that Christmas Eve. What made the difference was that for some reason Tricia actually beheld this person. He was seated under blinking colored lights in the doorway of a closed store, Erewhon Natural Foods, tucked into a corner that gave him some protection from the same wind that was biting through the gaps in Tricia's raccoon coat.

He did not have a coat, but was wrapped loosely in a thin, filthy blanket that had once been red, and that was still decorated with a hideous Santa head and "Ho, ho, ho" written in green and white. The blanket had slipped down from his shoulders to show a thin tee shirt, also filthy. His lips looked blue, though it could have been the lighting. He was probably middle-aged, but it was hard to tell with homeless people – most had the same furrowed, leathery skin, yellowed, bloodshot eyes, and matted hair.

She couldn't leave, but she wasn't sure how to help him. She just stood there at a distance of a few yards, remembering another Christmas Eve a long time past – she must have been eleven – the year she'd been selected for the youth choir to sing the midnight service at the church. She was at home an hour or so before the service, in the stuffy house, always too hot when the furnace was running, nearly always heavy with tension, and she'd escaped into the chill solitude of the enclosed front porch. Outside the walls of windows, snow-covered pines sparkled in starlight undimmed by streetlights on that country road. Huge icicles glittered from the porch eaves. On the windowsills, her mother had set electric candles in the Irish tradition, to welcome the traveler who could be an angel unaware. It was a relief to be alone with herself, yet not alone, but part of the story that spoke to her heart – of the angels and the poor, frightened shepherds who were bewildered as she was, the kings travelling through strange lands, and the star that led them to the child of their hope. She sang in full voice the carol she'd been practicing for the service:

Long lay the world in sin and error pining,
Till He appeared, and the soul felt its worth.

Her soul — was that what she was experiencing? She didn't know. She knew lights and light and something in her that opened into the cold infinity of the sky but did not feel cold. And though later that night she experienced the pine-decked church shining with candles, the life-sized crèche with the child's arms outstretched, the choir singing and the faithful gathered together – it was that earlier moment on the porch – that moment, and others like it, that had stayed with her through years of loneliness and darkness.

Now, on the street, she had another of those moments of clarity, in the company of this man in a desperate situation. She had a couple of coins in her pocket left over from buying groceries, but what he really needed was food. The casserole in her hands was still warm, and the Brothers wouldn't mind. She walked up to him.

"Hi," she said, handling him the pan. His hands as they brushed against hers were as cold as stone.

"No way!" he said. "The whole thing? Man!" He scooped up a handful and devoured it. "This is far out." He took another handful. "You're a good cook."

His speech wasn't slurred; in fact, he seemed pretty normal, at least for somebody who was freezing.

"Where do you live?" she asked, but oh no! the wrong question.

"Oh, you know. It isn't usually this cold out." He coughed, spitting some of the casserole onto his shirt.

She couldn't take him back to the house, with four single women trying to stay safe, and she hadn't heard of anyone bringing a homeless person to the Brother House.

As she wrapped her arms around herself against the wind, her raccoon coat was silky and comforting. It was a very old coat, one that her friend Luke had rescued in Buffalo years before when he was cleaning out a house after an old lady had died. It had ratty patches and the pelts were coming apart in places, but she liked it because it was real fur and vintage and part of the image she had created for herself.

"Are you going to be all right?" she asked. Another bad question.

"Yeah, sure. Thanks a lot, sister."

Sister. It was a term they all used – brother, sister, member of the movement, free spirit. But it sounded different just then.

She shrugged out of the coat and wrapped it around him. "Merry Christmas," she said, and started running toward home before the cold could hit her.

"Hey, wait, what –?"

"It's okay," she called back over her shoulder. And it was okay. She was home within ten minutes, took a bath, and slept. Like a baby, she thought when she woke the next morning, and smiled. She had a bit of a cold, but she went to the Brother House for the early service anyway.

CHAPTER SIX

Holy Communion?

Tricia – December 25, 1974

That Christmas morning Tricia attended her first Sunday service at the Brother House. The opening hymns included some she remembered from her Catholic upbringing, like "Praise Ye the Lord," and one she knew referred to the vision of Isaiah (another poetic book of Scripture she had often read) about the Lord being "high and lifted up and His train filled the temple." That much was fine. The sermon by Father Todd wasn't much different from his classes, urging them to change their lives and respond to the High Calling. But then the service began to resemble a Catholic Mass, and she became increasingly uncomfortable.

Father Todd stood before the altar to offer and, apparently, to consecrate bread and wine. The movements and even some of the words were familiar from years of attending Catholic Mass, as were the gleaming gold chalice and paten. But by what authority did he do this? By what ordination? Catholic bishops and priests claimed descent from the apostles, and so did the Episcopal and Lutheran clergy, but these? Of course, the Master Teachers had been given Divine Revelation about uniting all religions, but how did that involve Holy Communion? Her stomach knotted.

After the service, she approached Father Todd just as he was heading to the kitchen to get a cup of coffee, and pulled on his sleeve.

"Please, can I talk to you?"

"Tricia, have some mercy on a tired old man. It's Christmas, and I need some coffee and food."

"This is important. Really important."

Father Todd looked at her for a long moment, and then said, "Okay. Let's go back to the chapel since the rest of the house is full of people celebrating."

They sat on folding chairs facing each other.

"Okay, kid, what can't wait?"

"It's the communion, or the Holy Communion, whatever it is. I need to know what it is. Is it supposed to, I mean, is it – the Body and the Blood? Did Jesus say so when He appeared to Father Peter? Or is it something else, a commemoration or something?"

"Ahhhh, that. You were Catholic, weren't you?"

Tricia nodded. "I was until things didn't seem right anymore, and then I wasn't. Something didn't seem right with the communion today, either."

"So it's okay for you not to go to church for years and live however you happen to feel at the moment, but it's not okay to take Holy Communion?"

Tricia was getting used to Father Todd's sarcasm and didn't even flinch. "It's not okay to take Holy Communion unless it's Holy Communion."

"Okay, at least you have a conscience. Was the Catholic Holy Communion really Holy Communion?"

Good question. She hadn't thought about that since leaving the Catholic Church.

"I always believed it was, and I think it blessed me, but then the Catholic Church got all messed up, and I left. So I don't know anymore really. But Jesus gave the Holy Communion to the Apostles and the Apostles passed it on to the Church. And the Catholic Church says it's that same Church."

"Here's a question for you. Which is more important, the Church, or Jesus and the Apostles and the Holy Communion."

"Jesus, the Apostles, and the Holy Communion. Because the churches are all kind of messed up right now. Like they're not doing what they're supposed to be doing."

"I agree, but that's a different conversation for a different day. I'm going to tell you something, Tricia, but you can't go spreading it around, because a lot of people aren't ready for it, okay?"

Tricia nodded.

"You know that Jesus appeared many times to Father Peter, right?"

"Yes. To show him how to establish the Holy Order of Mystical Evangelists."

"Right. Do you want to know who Father Peter is, Tricia?"

She nodded, eyes wide.

"He is the Apostle Peter, reincarnated. You've been learning that all major religions are one. We are all reincarnated, some from very important people. It will take a long time for you to become Illuminated and Self-realized so you can understand who you are and who you have been. But all the Master Teachers are Apostles reincarnated."

Tricia stared at Father Todd, speechless. It was completely beyond understanding, but then so was any miracle, so were the apparitions to Father Peter, so was the idea that God knew who she was and had a plan for her. Bedazzled, she thanked Father Todd and joined the Christmas celebration with questions unanswered.

CHAPTER SEVEN

A Wrong-headed Kid in a Wrong-headed Town

Father Todd, February 1975

The Holy Order of Mystical Evangelists had handed Fr. Todd a mission in the most depraved place in the country, he was sure of it. In Lubbock, Texas where he had grown up, most people were basically sane. They went to church, went to work, got married, raised kids, watched football, and ate barbeque. Sure, there was more to life than that, and he was looking for it, but not the way folks in Berkeley, California were trying to "find themselves." He'd never seen such a place as this town for wrong-headed ideas. Able-bodied kids living on government handouts. Kids that were raised in church bowing to idols. Men with men and women with women, and calling it love. Free love. Ain't nothin free about love, as the country song sings it. If there's anything that costs plenty, it's love.

The White Brotherhood explained that they had selected Father Todd for this mission because he was too straight-talking to get sucked into the temptations. He had to laugh; he knew that by straight-talking they meant ornery, and he hoped they were right. The weather here was too perfect, the women weren't dressed to speak of, and nobody much cared what anybody else did – those were some temptations right there, but so far he was holding steady.

This poor little girl, Tricia, now – she'd been tossed back and forth by this place but good. Said she came here to get her life straight – say what? Could she have found a more messed up place if she tried? What actually happened was that she'd been fighting with herself, wanting God, wanting pleasure, wanting purpose, wanting an easy life. Where was her daddy, anyhow? Didn't he teach her any better? So she'd decided he, Father Todd, was her daddy, followed him around like a little puppy, watched his face to see if he liked what she said and did. Poor kid. It was okay with him, though. She'd be around here for just a little while longer before they'd get her into the novice program and give her some real structure for her life, some standards. It was no good talking about poems and changing the culture if you couldn't do a good day's work or keep a handle on how you were eating and drinking. Why, since he met her that girl had packed twenty pounds onto that little body of hers – maybe a fifth of her body weight – you'd wonder how she could carry it all around. You could tell she felt miserable in her body just by the way she walked, slowly and hesitantly, as if hoping nobody would notice her.

But then, in class, it was like she was a different person, all on fire to know whatever they could teach her. There was something in that kid that wanted to be self-realized, and he was going to do everything in his power to get her onto the path.

CHAPTER EIGHT

MISGIVINGS

Tricia, January and February 1975

Tricia's interior landscape was changing so fast it was hard to recognize herself. The conscious decisions she was making – to stop smoking pot and cigarettes, to pull back on drinking, to stop looking for love in the wrong places, to be purposely kind to people whether she liked them or not – all these were huge, and welcome. But beyond them were the unseen changes, the call and response going on deep in her psyche, changes she sensed but did not begin to understand. She was elated sometimes, yes, but she was also confused and really scared. And the more she tried to live a better life, the more she realized how flawed she was.

She set up a shrine in her bedroom using an inverted cardboard box covered with a scarf on which she placed a candle and a framed picture of Jesus that Brother Jarrell had given her. She knew that she needed to do more – she was actually supposed to pray at the shrine – but she hadn't actually prayed, as distinct from breathing and meditating, for years. How could she begin? With the old prayers from before? She didn't know any new ones.

One night she sat in front of the shrine, looked at the image of Jesus, took a deep breath, and just started talking.

"It's me. You know who I am. I'm sorry it's been so long. Please forgive me. I believe in you but I've felt so lost."

She studied the face in the picture. It was strong and serious, the face of somebody she had to tell the truth and no bull, and in that way it was fearful. But at the time moment, there was kindness in it. Tears ran down her face, not a sobbing kind of crying, but streaming, as if being washed from the inside out. She didn't say anything else, just sat there and wept. When the tears subsided, she felt weak, and lay down to sleep.

After that night, she would return to talk to Jesus a little more from day to day, sometimes using her own words, sometimes praying the Our Father, which she figured must be okay since Jesus gave it to people in the Gospel.

Not long afterward, though, she was trying to pray when one of her house mates in the next room started playing loud rhythm and blues. How outrageous that this "worldly music" was interrupting her prayers. Tricia knocked abruptly on her house mate's door.

Asia opened the door with a smile. "What's happening?"

"Asia, I'm trying to pray and it's impossible with this music. Can you turn it off for a while?"

Asia scowled. "No, I can't. Junior's over for the evening and we're dancing. It's Friday night, girl. Give me a break."

"Yeah, but what about me? I have a right to pray in my own home."

"Well, you do. And I have a right to dance in my own home." Asia nodded and closed the door.

Tricia knocked again, pounding this time, but there was no answer, just rhythm and blues, even louder now unless she was imagining it. Her face got hot and her heart beat faster. This was completely unjust. What was wrong with this girl? Didn't she have any respect? She ran out to the street, slamming the door, and walked to the Brother House. Brother Jarrell answered the door.

"Tricia, what are you doing here on a Friday night?"

"I can't pray at home. My stupid house mate won't turn down her music."

Brother Jarrell laughed gently. "Have a seat here on the porch."

Tricia pulled the rocking chair around so that she could face Brother Jarrell.

"It's just not fair. She's so mean."

"Tricia, listen to yourself. You want to pray, right?"

"Yes. I need to. I have to get ready to be baptized."

"And why do we pray?"

She was silent for a moment. "To be with God, right?"

"Yes. What else do we do to be with God?"

"Live right. Do what God says."

"And what does God say to do?"

"You know, the ten commandments."

"Okay, but the Master condensed the ten commandments into two. What are those?"

"Love God with all your heart, soul, mind, and strength, and …"

Brother Jarrell smiled teasingly. "And?"

"Love your neighbor as yourself. But Asia isn't loving me. She doesn't care how she's messing up my night."

"Are you responsible for what Asia does, or what you do?"

Tricia sighed.

"Maybe Asia doesn't understand how important your prayers are to you, but your job is to love her, not to call her stupid or be angry with her. Prayer doesn't have any place for anger. Do you see that?"

Tricia nodded. "I'm a hypocrite."

Brother Jarrell smiled. "You're a human being learning how to live. You just learned something important. Would you like to visit the chapel for a few minutes?"

She did, and prayer came easily, like it used to when she was a child.

*****

Tricia continued to spend time with Jana and Chad, who were beyond skeptical of her new involvement and did not hesitate to express their opinions. She staunchly defended HOME, while at the same time turning over in her mind her friends' arguments, along with the stricken sorrow of her Catholic mother and god-mother, both of whom she loved and trusted, and who were the first to bring up the term "cult" in relation to HOME.

In an attempt to free herself from "the establishment," or maybe because she wanted to spend all her time on matters she cared about more than current events, Tricia had not read newspapers or watched television for years. She hadn't been aware of the cult movement prevalent in the 1970's – the political and overtly dangerous Symbionese Liberation Army, or Sun Myung Moon's Unification Church which, like HOME, also attempted to unify all religions with a quasi-Christian message, but her godmother, her mother's sharp-witted sister who lived in Washington, D.C. and worked for the FBI, was very well informed and equated these cults with HOME. It seemed strange that her family, who had said next to nothing about her hedonistic lifestyle of the past few years, should be so upset now about her attempts to lead a life that served God and others. But then they had known little about the hedonism, and she couldn't stop telling them – or trying to tell them – about HOME.

Clearly she couldn't trust her family with the turmoil in her heart, and she couldn't trust Jana, who up until now had always been the first person she turned to. Praying didn't seem to be helping her confusion, either – it wasn't God she doubted, but herself, and maybe and maybe some of the practices in HOME, and she didn't know how to pray about that. How could she tell Brother Jarrell and Father Todd about her doubts and fears without damaging their faith in her? Instead, she stayed up late into the night when her house mates were asleep, sat beside the heater vent in the living room, shivering in the old, drafty house, and ate bowl after bowl of granola with milk. Nuts. Dried fruit. Bingeing on healthful food wasn't exactly bingeing, right? As long as her mouth was full she didn't have to think, she didn't have to feel. Between January and early March, she'd gained eighteen pounds.

One problem she did let herself think about, though, was what was happening with Daphne, a tall, blonde nineteen-year-old with a wide smile and perfect teeth, who was fascinated with plants and who seemed naïve and vulnerable even to Tricia.

One Sunday after services, Tricia and Daphne were taking a walk through People's Park. Daphne broke a sprig off one of the bushes, sniffed it, and held it under Tricia's nose.

"Oregano. Doesn't it smell good? Here, take it. You can make a tea from it with some ginger and black pepper, and it'll help you lose some of this weight you've been putting on."

Tricia blushed. "Is it that obvious?"

Willowy, graceful Daphne put her hand on Tricia's arm, newly padded with fat, and Tricia cringed.

"You're going through changes, sister. It's okay. But you don't want to keep carrying around more than you need, right?"

Tricia nodded sadly. She didn't feel like herself these days, not on the inside or on the outside.

"Look, over there – a whole row of hawthorn bushes – the berries are good for the heart," Daphne said. "You don't really find them much in L.A."

"Did you grow up in L.A.?" Tricia asked.

"Yes. We had an amazing house in Malibu, with a swimming pool and big terraces looking out to the ocean. Then my mom and dad split up, and she and I moved into an apartment in Encino. That was okay, until my mom decided to join an ashram."

"An ashram? Your mother? When did she do that?"

"A couple of years ago. It really stunk because I had to move back with my dad and leave all my friends and start at a new high school in the middle of my junior year. Those rich kids were so snobby; funny how I hadn't noticed when I was one of them. I wound up going to my senior prom with this guy I didn't know because his girlfriend got sick and nobody had asked me, so… you know. At least I got to go to the prom, though, right?" Daphne's wide grin had a touch of self-mockery.

"Was he nice?"

"Who?"

"The guy who took you to the prom."

"Oh, sure, he was okay. We really didn't know each other. He danced with me a couple times and then spent most of the night with his friends."

"What about you?"

Daphne shrugged. "I got to wear a pretty dress. Blue-green. My dad said it matched my eyes." She was silent for a moment, and then said, "It was okay to see more of my dad, but he was super busy with work most of the time."

"Did your mother stay at the ashram? Is she like a yogini or something?"

Daphne's mother had come to visit last month, but she didn't cry or plead or try to take Daphne home like some parents did. She acted as if she were on vacation, and maybe she was, flaunting designer sportswear, gold jewelry, heavy makeup, and a cloud of musk oil perfume. She flirted with any man in the room, including the Brothers. Tricia got the sense that Daphne hadn't had a mother she could turn to for a long time, if ever. Daphne seemed to have very little in common with this strange mother. Dressed in long cotton skirts and Indian blouses, she was fresh-faced, modest, friendly, and incredibly earnest.

Now Daphne laughed ruefully. "My mom isn't big on discipline, Tricia. She stayed there for a while. Then she went to India for a couple months with some man she'd met. When she came back, she didn't seem too interested in anything spiritual. But it didn't make sense to move back in with her, especially since the guy she was living with gave me the creeps. That's when I came to Berkeley. I went to classes at CAL for a semester, and then I met Father Todd in Sproul Plaza. Can you believe this – I saw his long monk's robe and asked him if he was with the Society for Creative Anachronism!"

Tricia and Daphne caught each other's eyes and burst out laughing, hugging each other and laughing helplessly.

When they caught their breath, Tricia said, "I haven't laughed like that since I got to Berkeley."

Daphne wiped her eyes. "I needed that. I've had a lot on my mind. Tricia, I have to tell you something. Will you promise not to tell anyone, not anyone at all?"

"Uh oh. I don't know. Did you murder somebody?"

"Right. I guess I am getting a little heavy. But this is so important, and I've got to talk to somebody I trust."

"And you trust me because…?"

"Because you're older, and you're serious about things, and you're kind to me."

"I guess I'm kind to you because I like you. You know, I may be twenty-two but that doesn't mean I know what I'm doing all the time."

Daphne shrugged. "Will you keep my secret?"

"Okay. Shoot."

Daphne looked up, looked down, looked Tricia in the eyes and said, "Father Todd and I are in love."

Tricia sank down on a park bench while thoughts flew through her mind. She'd be a hypocrite to judge Daphne for this, considering her own feelings for Brother Jarrell. She dreamed of being life-vowed and maybe someone he would want to marry. But right now these Brothers of Holy Poverty were on mission, and under a special vow. While all members of the Holy Order of Mystical Evangelists had taken vows of purity – defined as right relationship with God and others – the dedicated Brothers of Holy Poverty and the dedicated Sisters of Mercy belonged to special sub-orders within the Brotherhood and had taken an additional temporary vow of celibacy. Celibacy in this case meant not only the sexual abstinence it means to most people – which was always required outside of marriage – but giving up any special, close relationship with any person, no matter how chaste. The celibate brother or sister had to be detached even from particular friendships, not to speak of courtships, and instead had to concentrate only on prayer and service. Brother Jarrell always treated Tricia with brotherly kindness, but he never got personal, and outwardly neither did she.

"In love with each other? He said he's in love with you too?"

"Yes." Her lovely young face was beaming. "We both felt it right away when we met last year, but neither one of us said anything. Father Todd spoke to me about it only two months ago, after he'd had a revelation that we are destined to be together. You know he is Self-Realized, so it must be a revelation from God."

"Really? Why would God tell him to break his vow?"

"Oh, Tricia, we've never done anything but hug and kiss and talk about the future."

"I hope not! But that's still breaking his vow. He's not supposed to be hugging and kissing and talking about a future with you. He's on mission."

Daphne was silent for a while. Then, "I thought you'd understand."

"Daphne, I understand that Father Todd is wise and funny and good-looking and kind, and I don't blame you for feeling the way you do. But he's the head of this mission group, and he has a responsibility to all of us, including me, including you."

Daphne sighed. "Yes, of course. We've talked about that. That's why we're not telling people. We want to do everything right. We'll have to be patient, wait for the mission to run its course, and for me to become life-vowed. Then we can be married." Daphne's huge blue eyes widened with sincerity. She was living in her own fairy tale, in which a powerful, handsome prince was going to carry her off to his castle – a holy castle in a holy order no less – and she would live happily ever after.

"I just had to talk with somebody. Maybe you don't understand, but you're still my friend, right? You won't tell anyone, will you?"

"Yes, of course I'm still your friend and no, I won't tell anyone. You can trust me. But it doesn't feel right. For another thing, Father Todd is a lot older than you."

"I'm nineteen; I'm an adult."

Tricia wanted to remind Daphne that she still called this man Father, but she only shrugged. Argument wasn't going to help any here.

"I hope it works out for you."

Daphne gave Tricia a weak smile and started to talk about how drinking Chai could help with weight loss. She'd brew some for Tricia for next Wednesday's class.

Tricia was barely listening. She couldn't help feeling that Father Todd, who should have known better, was cheating. And spiritual guides shouldn't cheat. These thoughts occupied her for the rest of that day and then that night, as she sat beside the heating vent in the dark again.

Tricia's mother had trusted her parish priest to help her deal with a husband who beat his wife and children – a man who now might be called a dry alcoholic or a rage-a-holic, who served as an usher at the parish church and then backed his wife into the corner of the hallway with a broom, or threw his oldest daughter, Tricia – a strong-willed, defiant child as he said – down the cellar stairs. Tricia was pretty sure he had broken her nose that day, though no one really noticed and so it healed crooked, only one among many reasons that people called her attractive, but not beautiful. While he was beating her, Tricia would keep telling herself, don't cry, don't let him get to you. If he hurts you badly enough, maybe somebody will find out and help.

Some time later, when her mother tried to talk to the parish priest about the situation, he told her to be a good wife and submit to her husband. Then he put his hand on her knee and put his arm around her. Her mother told Tricia, who was thirteen, that she didn't know what to do in that moment. Tricia, who had never even been on a date, had no suggestions. What her mother had cleverly decided was to get up from the couch and make coffee for her reverend guest, hoping to break the mood. She never tried to talk to him again.

But untrustworthy priests were not the biggest part of Tricia's Catholic upbringing. There were also the quiet mornings in the candlelit church, praying the litanies. Seat of Wisdom pray for us. Mystical Rose, pray for us. Morning Star pray for us. Poetry – pure, ethereal poetry in the flickering light of dozens of candles. In wonder. In peace. In safety. Tricia had felt whole during those prayers. And then the services changed to a people-centered dialog with guitars, and she changed, and she left it. Where was wonder now? Where were peace and safety? She had to find another way. Maybe she had. But maybe not. And so in this way even her concern for Sister Daphne morphed into concern for herself and added to the hundreds of voices in her mind, and she ate another bowl of granola.

In spite of the fact that someone who doesn't believe in much of anything at all probably doesn't have a great perspective on matters of faith, Jana had a point about integrity. Tricia certainly didn't want to take some easy way out of facing how hard life is or avoid having an authentic response to it. Whatever road she took would have to be the best she could find, even if it was the hardest. But how was she supposed to decide? Did she have to decide? Who said that even if we don't make a decision, we've still made a choice? Her world had been full of people who seemed to just let life happen to them. She didn't want to be one of those people.

CHAPTER NINE

A Sheep to the Slaughter

Jana, Berkeley, March 1975

Tricia was Jana's best friend, not because Tricia was thoughtful and kind, because she wasn't especially thoughtful or kind. She was too self-absorbed to be thoughtful, and often too obsessed with figuring out her own life to be consistently kind. She was randomly kind, because she had a basically good heart that would sometimes tell her to help out someone else, but you could never rely on her. Jana would tell her something really important, like about her own heart, like how she thought she was maybe in love with her professor at State but it would never work out, and Tricia wouldn't remember it the next time they talked. Jana would ask Tricia to take care of her plants while she was away, and she'd forget and let them die. She never remembered Jana's birthday unless Jana dropped a hint the day before. So she always dropped a hint the day before, because Tricia was her best friend and Jana needed for her to remember the birthday.

The main reason Tricia was Jana's best friend was that Tricia wanted to know the truth about things, about everything. She wanted to be real, and so did Jana. The first time they met in high school

53

they saw that they each wanted this more than anything. More than the guys they loved and lost. More than the art and beauty they followed after like starving people. More than sleep, for sure, because they would sit up all night reading and talking and asking questions and trying to answer them. They trusted that desire in each other, even through the dark days after Jonathan left Tricia and joined the Navy and she spiraled into a place Jana wasn't sure she would escape. But even then, Tricia kept reading and writing and asking questions, even if that itself was making her kind of crazy.

Gradually, the questions Jana was asking made her more skeptical of just about everything except maybe a spark of good in most people, and the value of doing some good in this weird and puzzling world before that spark in her went out. She'd finished college with a major in special education, and wound up liking her simple-hearted students. Tricia said that Jana was a humanist, and maybe she was. What was wrong with that? People were important. But the questions Tricia was asking led her away from people and apparently into other worlds. For a while Jana became a kind of guardian for her, until the job became too much.

One day Tricia came home waving a notebook and announcing, "I found an answer!" It turned out she'd been reading anthropology and comparative religions and discovered a thread of revelation running through the pre-Christian religions. Okay, Jana thought. Tricia sounded unhinged but what else was new? At least it made her happy, and she stopped taking drugs and started eating again, even though she was always in her room writing, which was kind of a drug in its own right, and so after a while she started getting too skinny again. She wasn't sleeping much – no surprise. How could anybody hold two millennia of revelation in her head, and how was a person who hadn't finished her B.A. – even a self-proclaimed visionary who hadn't completed her B.A. – supposed to communicate all that to the world? But that was what Tricia was attempting all day and night shut up in her room. If Jana and Tricia's sister,

Rita, hadn't brought her food sometimes she wouldn't have eaten for days.

That was about the time Jana graduated and her boyfriend, Chad, wanted for them to move from Buffalo all the way across the country to Santa Cruz, California. Jana thought a long time before she agreed to leave Tricia, but what could she actually do? She had to admit that she wasn't really helping her, just supporting the insanity. She applied for a teaching job in San Jose, a reasonable commute from Santa Cruz, and when she got an an offer, she accepted it.

Not long after, Tricia decided to move to Berkeley to write poetry and make a different life for herself. A more creative life, she said on the phone when she called. Berkeley wasn't very far from Santa Cruz, so they got together from time to time. The first time Tricia came to visit Jana and Chad, they took her to the beach, where she immediately stripped down to underwear and a tee shirt, and ran headlong into the water, not thinking about the fact that it was January and this was northern California. She got bad hypothermia – shaking, teeth chattering, blue extremities. They wrapped her in all their coats, rushed her back to the house, dumped her into a warm bath, and pumped her with tea. That was Tricia, though – always some drama.

They talked on the phone fairly often, and she told Jana about her poetry, the occasional reading at an open mike, collecting unemployment while working now and then as a prep cook, doing yoga at the YMCA with a friend. There were a couple of guys she'd mention from time to time, but nothing serious – guys never stayed with Tricia very long – too intense they'd say. She lived with some pretty reasonable women as house mates, though, and she seemed to be getting more stable. At least her life allowed for relationships and exercise for a change, if not a way to make a living.

Then she met these HOME loonies. The first conversation went something like this:

"Jana, I think I've found a better way to live."

"Oh yeah? Even better than being a prep cook for minimum wage when you're one of the smartest people in that crazy city of yours?"

"Come on, Jana. I'm not talking about making money. I've found a way to become a better person and make the world a better place."

"Tricia, you're a pretty good person already, and if you try you can be better. What you need right now is some useful work to do, to take you out of your own head. You live right down the street from the best public university in the country, and it's cheap. Why don't you go back to school and finish what you dropped out of?"

Audible sigh. "You know how I feel about that. School's okay for reading great literature and writing about it, but the last thing I need is to focus on a degree and lose myself in some job and wake up one day at sixty wondering what happened to my life. I have to become myself. Then I can write something worth reading, and give something to the world."

"Uh huh. Something more valuable than teaching kids or making people well, right?"

"Jana, I'm not criticizing the work you and Chad do. It's great how you can help those kids. And Chad must come home from the hospital every day happy he's provided care to suffering people. But I have something different to do, and I think I've finally found the way to it."

"So what is it?"

Silence.

"Well?"

"Okay, just let me talk a little before you interrupt me. All right?"

"Agreed."

"I've found a spiritual order –"

"Son of a –!

"Jana, you promised."

"Okay, okay. You found a religious order. What? You're going to become a nun all of a sudden? Do they know who you are?"

"No. Not a religious order, a spiritual order, The Holy Order of Mystical Evangelists. Now, I'm going to describe it and you're going to be quiet, all right?"

"Yeah, all right."

But Jana was already angry, not with poor, mixed up Tricia who thought she was going to save the world by writing poetry (If I could just tell people what I SEE, she was always saying, as if her life was working out great because of what she SAW). Jana was angry with whoever was taking advantage of Tricia now, as others had in the past, because in so many ways Tricia hadn't even started to grow up yet. But she'd promised to listen, so she lit a cigarette, took a deep drag, and listened.

"It's called the Holy Order of Mystical Evangelists, HOME for short, or just The Order. It was started by a man named Father Peter who used to be a priest but was tired of the problems of organized religions. He had a revelation from God –"

"Stop right there," she blurted out.

"No. You're going to listen. He had a revelation that he should gather chosen people to help the world enter a New Age of enlightenment by becoming Illumined and Self-Realized themselves and helping others to do the same."

Jana was tapping her foot and dragging like mad on the cigarette, but she didn't say anything yet.

"So he found five other people and brought them to Self-Realization. These are the Master Teachers. And they have all called disciples to themselves and are bringing them through Illumination and Self-realization, to make a better world."

Sometimes when she knew Jana wouldn't agree with what she was saying, Tricia would talk fast to get it all out before Jana could object. Now, though, she was talking very slowly, enunciating every word, as if talking to a little child, or an idiot. It was really annoying.

"But they don't just pray and meditate and work on themselves, they do a lot of service work with alcoholics and addicts and street people. They take vows of poverty, purity, obedience, humility, and service. So it's kind of like being a monk or a nun, but living in the world, which is something I wanted to do when I was a teenager but the Catholic pastor told me I couldn't, that I'd have to either get married or be a nun. People in this Order can stay single or get married, and they have jobs, even careers, and still do all kinds of prayer and service. Okay, Jana, I know you're dying, so go ahead and ask your questions."

"How do you know this father person had a revelation from God? Don't you think that's a little unusual? Do you know who else hears God talking to them? People with schizophrenia and bipolar disorder. Or what you might understand better, people who are possessed."

"As if you believed in people being possessed."

"That doesn't matter, you do. And I do believe in people, lots of people these days, having mental disorders. And guess what? Some of them have started their own religions. And right here in California, too."

"So I think there was a question in there somewhere, and I'll answer it. I've gotten to know some of the people from HOME, and I trust them. They study the Bible, and they pray to the Holy Trinity just like Catholics or Protestants, but they don't have all the rules and judgements and fears. They're free children of God, and they're becoming more enlightened every day. I want to do that."

"Fine. Me too. I want to be enlightened and kind and shine like a freaking star in the sky, but that doesn't mean I should listen to somebody who's hearing voices."

"Saints heard voices, Jana."

"And you're saying all these people are saints?"

"No, but maybe Father Peter had a pure heart and God spoke to him and gave him a mission."

Jana knew she couldn't argue with Tricia's God talk, so she'd have to try something else. "Maybe. Say that's true. What makes you think it's your mission?"

"Because they're doing what I've wanted to do for a long time – they're becoming enlightened and making a better culture, a better world. That's why I came to Berkeley, to be part of that. And now I can."

"Tell me this: did those saints you're talking about make a better world? Or Buddha? Or Mother Teresa?"

Silence from Tricia.

"No," Jana went on. "They became good people and did a little good where they could. That's about all anybody can do."

Tricia was silent.

"Trish, you know I love you."

She lit another cigarette and waited.

Finally, "I know you love me. And I love you. But you just don't get it, Jana, and maybe you never will. I've got to go get ready for class. We'll talk soon."

And they did talk soon; when Tricia told her she was going to be "baptized," Jana jumped into the car right after work that Friday night and drove to Berkeley, where they had an intense talk on a stone wall on Telegraph Avenue and Tricia talked – again – about two roads, and Jana talked – again – about opening her eyes and seeing what was in front of her.

A lot of good that did. And soon it would be too late.

CHAPTER TEN

BAPTISM TWO?

Tricia/Althea, April 1975

Tricia knelt before the altar as Father Todd pressed his open palms hard against the top of her head. His hands were vibrating – was it from the force of her transformation? Was power passing through him and into her? Or were his arms just shaking from the exertion of pressing into her skull? Did these questions she was always asking mean her faith was weak?

They called this first initiation "Baptism," though it didn't have much in common with the Baptism Tricia had received as a baby and learned about later in Catholic grade school. This second of her baptisms seemed to have less to do with water and the Spirit than with energy. "The Light," they called it. They were supposed to be receiving The Light, to keep receiving it until they became Illumined (the second initiation) and then Self-Realized (the final step in becoming godlike.) At the moment, Tricia was trying hard to see The Light. Of course she could see light – sunlight streaming through the bay window of the living room of the cottage this April morning of 1975 – glorious, golden rays of light – but it didn't look any more or less heavenly than sunlight always did.

Was this *The Light* that was gradually transforming them into Self-Realized beings of light? That was another of those questions she was always asking.

Father Todd's eyes were closed tightly and his head was tilted back with concentration. Surely something spiritual was happening. Jana was here, though hugging the back wall, close to the door. Would Jana finally begin to understand? Tricia was surprised that her friend had come, since she suspected any religion, not to mention one that embraced Christianity as this one Tricia had chosen, and one so new and different that most people were skeptical about it. In fact, some of the initiates' parents had forcibly removed their sons and daughters from training and had them professionally un-brainwashed or whatever it was called. The Brothers shook their heads as they told those stories, marveling at how much suffering was caused by those who couldn't believe. But though Jana didn't have faith, she loved Tricia, and Tricia treasured that.

Father Todd's hands were vibrating hard now, as if an electrical current were passing through him. Was it passing through Tricia? She couldn't tell, probably because she was too dense and earthly.

"You shall be called…" His voice, weighty with authority, filled the still room and then paused while he listened for the name that would be revealed to him. Her head rocked beneath his palms.

"…Althea."

Althea. She would be Althea now. She would miss her name, but this was part of letting go of the old person she had been. To be someone entirely new. A spiritual person. A person with a mission.

She caught a flash of movement to her left and glanced over in time to see Jana running from the room with her head turned down into her shoulder as if she were crying. Tricia/Althea wanted to go after her, but she couldn't very well leave in the midst of her own Baptism.

Father Todd took her hands and lifted her to her feet.

"Rise, Althea," he said. "Our sister."

It was kind of him to say she was a sister, because she really wasn't yet. She'd been initiated through this Baptism, but hadn't taken vows yet – the vows of poverty, purity, humility, obedience, and service – not even the temporary vows of a student. Until she took her final vows in two years or more, she wouldn't really be part of the Brotherhood, not really a Sister, though as a student she would be called "Sister." It was confusing. But she did feel welcomed as Father Todd gave her a shoulder hug. She let go into the strength of his fatherly arm and laid her head against the rough brown wool of his sleeve. He was proud of her.

Father Todd wasn't quite old enough to be her father, but she thought he was often wise enough, and ever since she'd first visited the Brother House for a class nearly four months before, he'd treated her as if she were his spiritual daughter. He thought nothing of ridiculing her misconceptions, which he said were really the world's misconceptions that she'd foolishly absorbed. The values, or lack thereof, that she had absorbed from the late sixties and early seventies had left her confused about so many things.

"Just forget about men right now," he's advised. "Go through your novitiate and your student training. Become Illumined. Then you can marry a good man and the two of you can serve together."

That had sounded fine to Tricia. High purpose and love. Very fine indeed.

"Come forward and greet Althea," he said now, extending his hands to the congregation.

The dozen or so people who crowded the small living room chapel came forward one at a time to hug and congratulate her. There was Brother Ronald – shy, kind, and tongue-tied, who held a day job at a local library. Then there was Brother Vince, a wiry carpenter with a quick wit and a fiery temper who was the house steward for the four-man mission team. A number of people who regularly attended services and classes had come for the initiation, too, including Georgie, who had been baptized a long while before, but wasn't planning to join the Brotherhood. She gave Tricia a big squeeze.

"You're beautiful, kiddo," she said. "That angel robe is a nice touch."

"It's not an angel robe, Georgie," she said, nudging her house mate and rolling her eyes. Tricia was wearing a long, unbleached muslin dress her sister Rita had made her when she'd begun to dress like a hippie a couple of years before, though she'd added a blue leotard underneath to modify the low neckline. She'd washed her long brown hair that morning and blow-dried it with her head upside-down so it would fan out around her head. She felt beautiful, and she wanted to feel beautiful, but she was cautious about being vain.

"It's just a dress, the best one I've got."

"Well, you look like an angel anyhow. Or a saint."

Althea shook her head to drive away the spiritual pride, far worse than vanity, which liked hearing these things said about her.

"You're going to look better in black, though."

Novices and students wore black clerical garb, a lot like a nun's or seminarian's, street length dresses for the women, shirts and slacks for the men, and Roman collars.

"I wish you'd come along, Georgie. It doesn't seem fair for you to bring me this far and then say good-bye."

"No, no. Too holy for my blood. I'm not up to spreading the truth. I just want to keep from going down there," she said, laughing, tossing her bleached curls, and pointing to the floor. "I went down in a burning ring of fire," she sang, and laughed again.

Althea found out later that Georgie had wanted for years to join The Brotherhood, but she hadn't been accepted – something about her not being teachable enough for HOME. It made Tricia sad when she heard that. It seemed that Georgie's good heart must have been stronger than all the scars from bad relationships, drugs, alcohol, or whatever else she had been through and left behind.

The last person to congratulate Althea was Brother Jarrell. What a tall, slim poet he was. His resting face often betrayed pain, probably because of how sensitive he was to the sufferings of the world, and especially to ugliness in any form. He was someone who should always be surrounded by beauty.

"You're like a bouquet of fresh flowers," Brother Jarrell said to her as he gave her a one-armed hug, and for a moment she lost her breath. Then she reminded herself again – he loved her only in the same compassionate way he loved everybody. He was taking his role as a dedicated Brother of the Holy Light very seriously. He represented what she now believed a man should be, but she really knew very little about him. Even she realized that she was a lonely young woman drawn to someone who was kind to her.

When she looked up into the fine, pained features of Brother Jarrell's face, he smiled and nodded his support of her calling. His face was so bright to her eyes. Was this The Light?

CHAPTER ELEVEN

ANDROMEDA

Jana, April 1975

If you took a Catholic baptism and crossed it with a wedding at an ashram, you might get some picture of what Tricia subjected herself to at her so-called "Baptism." There was a "priest" in a long white robe, there was an altar, a truckload of incense, candles, and flowers, and more than a dozen attendees chanting with glazed looks in their eyes.

Jana's eyes were not glazed. She could see everything too clearly. Tricia, her best friend who used to be an honors student at the state college until she dropped out, who was one of the smartest people she knew except when she wasn't, who insisted she believed in God and Jesus, was kneeling in front of this voodoo altar with a fake priest chanting over her, putting his hands on her, for all Jana knew sucking the soul out of her.

The "brothers," three guys dressed up in monk robes as if it were Halloween, looked on, smiling and nodding. The tall, thin one must be the angelic Brother Jarrell Tricia was always talking about. He did have a kind face and an ethereal look about him, but he had the same glazed look in his eyes that they all did.

Jana had to admit that Tricia herself looked better than she had in a long time, except for the weight she'd gained so suddenly. Besides that, and the glazed eyes, her face was fresh, and she was smiling. She had told Jana she'd been cleaning up her act – no smoking, no parties, no male drama. She had dressed for the ceremony in a long white dress with blue at the throat and sleeves and a crown of blue flowers on her head. She looked something like a bride, and something like Andromeda about to be sacrificed to the monster. That was one of Tricia's favorite myths, one she identified with – a girl chained to a rock by her messed up father – but where was Perseus who was supposed to save her? There had never been a Perseus for Tricia.

The fake priest still had his hands on her head, and his arms were shaking as he looked up to the ceiling. Oh, brother. The room became absolutely silent. And now he was saying something in a booming voice, something unimaginable:

"You shall be called – Althea!"

No! Jana's stomach clenched into a knot and tears of fury stung her eyes. They were taking her name from her. Her *name*. What right did they have to do that? She loved her name, short for Patricia, after Patrick, the shepherd who sat under the stars and prayed until he had the strength to run away from slavery, who had the guts to come back to the Irish who'd held him captive and tried to help them. She'd told Jana the story a dozen times. Jana was ambivalent about saints, but Patrick was one great human being and Tricia was named after him – until just now.

Jana couldn't stay there another minute, and made for the door. Tricia turned to see her leave at the same moment Tricia left her.

CHAPTER TWELVE

A Visit "HOME"

Althea – April 1975

"The Bay Bridge is some crazy feat of engineering," Father Todd said, glancing at Althea sideways as he drove.

She realized she hadn't said much of anything since they'd left the Berkeley Brother House, that her thoughts had been racing ahead to her imminent first visit to the HOME center in San Francisco.

"Is she kind?" Althea asked.

"Who?"

"The one in charge of the novices."

"Reverend Ursula? Kind? I don't think that's something she's particularly known for, or even tries to be. She's self-realized, strong, and wise. I think she's fair. You want somebody strict enough to make you change and grow, don't you?"

It seemed a rhetorical question so Althea went silent again as Father Todd drove into the city, through the busy downtown area, then through a wasteland of dilapidated buildings and freeway overpasses, and finally into a neighborhood of old but still lovely Victorian houses painted in rainbow colors.

"Here we are," Father Todd announced. "You're HOME now!"

She was expected to laugh, but she only nodded. It wasn't funny then, and it wasn't funny the hundreds of times she heard it afterward. In fact, it made her cringe. She hated puns, and she couldn't see how people could joke about something as holy as the name of a spiritual order founded on Divine revelation. It was often hinted that she wasn't spiritually enlightened enough to be playful.

The house they approached was freshly painted in white with blue trim, very conservative compared with the yellow and purple one or the red and orange one on the same block. The front stairs were steep and the door was narrow. The woman who answered the door was wearing a simple, knee-length black dress, a wooden cross, and a Roman collar like Father Todd's. She stood at least a head taller than Tricia, with a muscular physique and erect posture. Her light brown hair was pulled back into a French twist and secured with a barrette. She wore no make-up – none of the sisters did – but she had remarkable porcelain skin and clear blue eyes. Her demeanor was calm. She did not smile.

In fact, Reverend Ursula reminded Althea of a porcelain nun doll her mother's aunt, a Catholic nun, had given her mother when she was a child in the 1920's. Doll makers then seemed to have a different idea of what a woman is. That porcelain woman was tall and substantial, powerful, with a serene, unsmiling face and wise-looking blue glass eyes. She was not so much beautiful as noble, and she modelled for Tricia a woman very different from Barbie and high fashion dolls – one who was strong and courageous. This woman in front of her apparently was both, as well as being as stiff and cold as a porcelain doll.

She nodded to Father Todd, and fixed her eyes intently on Tricia. "You must be Patricia. I am Reverend Ursula, your novice master."

"Tricia."

"What's that?"

"My name is Tricia. No one ever calls me Patricia."

Reverend Ursula's thick, dark eyebrows drew together, but before she could speak, Father Todd came to the rescue.

"That won't matter anymore, will it? You are Althea now. You will be called Althea. Sister Althea."

Reverend Ursula gave a curt nod, and stepped aside to allow them to enter a dark, narrow Victorian hallway. As they proceeded through the first two floors of the house, she explained the living arrangements.

"This building houses the resident Master Teachers on the top floor. We have two living here now, Master Matthew and Master Aphrodite-Maria, who are married to each other. The priests and life-vowed Brothers and Sisters live on the second floor. Our common areas and offices are on the first floor. The main chapel and garden are on the level below us. You will be attending services in the main chapel only on Sundays and for special events. Otherwise you will be in the novice chapel where I will serve."

They followed her back to the front door and across the street to another, smaller Victorian house painted in the same white and blue.

"The novice quarters are in this house," she continued. "It has a separate kitchen and dining room, a small chapel, and a laundry room that serves the whole community."

As they walked, she also explained that the life-vowed Brothers and Sisters had jobs, some right here at the center such as the cook and the bursar, but most in the city as teachers, nurses, secretaries, laborers, and office workers, using any skills they had brought with them when they joined the Holy Order of Mystical Evangelists. Some had returned to school to finish degrees abandoned when they "dropped out" of the "establishment culture." One talented young woman was even attending medical school. This news appealed to Althea, since she had left college twice to "find herself" and she wanted to complete her BA in English.

But Reverend Ursula made it plain that the prospect of finishing school was far in the future, at such time as Althea became life-vowed, if that happened. In between stretched a transformation period – a three-month novitiate, a year of student training, a year of renunciate service with The Sisters of Mercy and a period of testing to discern whether she was called to this life.

In a few weeks' time, she would begin the novitiate. A novice, said Reverend Ursula, is like the Fool of the Tarot deck – all innocence and potential, ready to step off the edge of this present life in the world, trusting that something greater will keep him from falling. A novice's virtue, the only one that can be expected of a person so unattained, is obedience. Every day – nearly every hour – of the novice's life is scheduled and supervised. A novice leaves the Old Man at the door and begins the process of becoming a new creature.

Because Althea had aunts who were Catholic nuns, she knew that this kind of extreme isolation during a novitiate was not unusual in an established religious order. Probably HOME was basing the practice on Catholic monasticism, and she didn't know, had no way of knowing, though the mention of the Tarot deck might have alerted her, that its goals were not entirely the same. She did know that this was not a monastery, since life-vowed brothers and sisters had not left the world exactly. They courted, married, and had children. They worked at regular jobs and had social lives. It was difficult to face how restricted her life was going to be. She hoped she wasn't too spiritually dense for this life.

The tour ended back at the main house, where Reverend Ursula seated them on a couch in a comfortable living room. She took a chair opposite, sat erect on the edge, and folded her hands in her lap.

"What questions do you have, Pa–, eh, Althea?" she asked, leaning slightly forward.

"Do the novices ever visit this main house?" Althea asked, admiring the sun streaming though the bay window.

"As I explained earlier, they attend Sunday services in the main chapel," she answered crisply, "and, of course, as part of their training, they have the opportunity to serve the life-vowed community who live here in various capacities as part of their training."

"Do the novices have their own library then?" This room was lined with floor to ceiling bookshelves, well-stocked. She wanted to get her hands on some of those titles.

"During the novitiate there is much to do and much to learn. Reading time is limited and reading materials are assigned –"

Althea gasped audibly at this, and Father Todd, whom she was beginning to think of as her true and only friend in this alien environment, hastened to add, "But that's only for three months. Students and life-vowed brothers and sisters are encouraged to read broadly."

Althea breathed again. "What about visitors?" She had been hoping that Jana would get over whatever had sent her running out of the Baptism initiation and come to see her, even start to see the Order differently. Anything was possible. And then there was her mother who had been so concerned; maybe she would want to visit to be sure her daughter was all right.

Reverend Ursula and Father Todd exchanged a look which Althea was sure she was not meant to notice. It was Father Todd who spoke, no doubt because he knew she trusted him.

"No visitors are allowed during the novitiate," he said gravely. "A novice needs to be immersed in the new life, without any distractions from the outside."

"Okay," she said after a moment's thought. "But we can receive phone calls, right?"

He shook his head.

"Letters?"

He answered in his broadest drawl, with his biggest smile, not just from his mouth but from his eyes. "Sister Althea, you are going to dedicate yourself completely to your new life, to the High Calling. You are going to need to let go of everyone and everything you have ever known, not forever in most cases, but for now, to break your attachment to your old life. Do you think you are up to that?"

Althea wasn't sure whether it was her own conviction and commitment or a desperate need for his approval which prompted her to swallow and slowly nod assent.

"Good girl," Father Todd beamed. "You're going to look great in black."

CHAPTER THIRTEEN

SHE CAN'T HEAR ME ANYMORE

Melissa Schwartz Riley, May 1975

Melissa Schwartz Riley sat at the kitchen table chain-smoking and drinking coffee. She wasn't eating or sleeping well lately. How could she, when her daughter was about to betray her faith and throw away her life?

She and Tricia had always been so close. Tricia had told her everything and called her a confidante, not just when she was little, but as she matured, even for a while after she left home. She'd written every week while she was travelling through Europe to tell her mother about the wonders and the struggles – the charming young architect who took her dancing at an outdoor pavilion, the light on the old stone walls in Reggio Emilia, the issues with her travelling companion who decided they had to leave Milan before Tricia could attend the opera *Aida* in the Colosseum, the way the air in the Italian Alps smelled so delicious she could eat it. Melissa could almost live all of it through those letters. That wasn't so very long ago. Even though Tricia had left home, part of her was always with her mother. Until now.

Now they had phone calls that lasted only a couple of minutes before Tricia went silent. The last call went something like this:

"I can take the train to California next month. It's been so long since we've seen each other," Melissa said.

"Mom, don't come. I won't be able to see you."

"What do you mean?"

Her daughter sighed audibly. "I'll be going to the Holy Order House to start novice training in two weeks."

"And? You don't have to put me up. I can stay at a hotel."

"Mom, I can't have visitors."

"What? They won't let you see your mother?"

"I can't have any visitors for the first three months, during my novitiate. It would be the same way in a Catholic convent."

"Maybe, but this isn't a Catholic convent and you are not becoming a nun. What are they doing for those three months that they don't want anybody to know about?"

Silence.

"Tricia?"

"Mom, my name is Althea now."

"What! They changed your name!"

"Not 'they' Mom, 'I.' I changed my name. Well, actually I accepted the name that was given me."

"Given by…?"

"By God. By God."

"Honey! Please, go talk with a priest. You are in delusion. God did not give you a new name. God does not go around giving people new names."

"Of course He does, Mom. He gave Abram/Abraham a new name, and Jacob/Israel, and Simon/Peter, and Saul/Paul.

"They were saints, honey."

"Not before He gave them a new name. And my own aunts were given new names when they became nuns.

"By their abbess, not by God."

"And God doesn't speak through the abbess?"

"Oh, God help me, I could never win an argument with you!...

Silence.

"Honey?"

"Yes."

"Say something."

"Like what, Mom? If I explain, we'll just argue like before. You don't understand what I'm doing, and it's useless to keep trying to make you understand."

"Honey, what's useless is you throwing your life away like this. You know I'm an educated person, and an open-minded person, don't you?"

"Yes. Yes, you are both. I mean, you are usually open-minded."

"I'm a college graduate. I had a good job as an accountant before I married. I know you're very smart, Tricia, but I'm smart too, and if your arguments made any sense, I think I would understand them."

Silence. A long silence.

"Tricia, honey – or whatever they call you – please talk to me."

"I really don't have anything else to say."

"Has anyone you look up to or trust accepted your arguments?"

Silence.

"Well?"

"I'm not making arguments, Mom. I believe. It's a matter of faith."

"Faith? What about your Catholic faith?"

A loud sigh. Then silence.

"You had a Catholic faith, honey. We baptized you when you were a month old – your Aunt Helen was your godmother. And she came for your first Holy Communion when you were seven – on May 22nd – it will be only sixteen years ago this month. And you were confirmed as a Catholic when you were twelve." Melissa's voice became shrill. "I just can't understand why you would abandon your faith now. You say you've been "baptized" again, but why would you need to be baptized again?"

But the more that Melissa objected, the more silent her daughter became.

"I have to go now, Mom. This call is costing you a lot of money and we're not communicating."

Melissa was weeping silently. "We need to reach some resolution, honey. Especially if we won't be able to speak again for months."

"What would you call resolution, Mom?"

Now Melissa had no words.

"I love you, Mom. That hasn't changed."

"And I love you, honey, always."

That was the end of their conversation. And yes, their love for each other was at least something of a resolution, something she could hold onto. But how was Melissa supposed to accept that this "order" wouldn't even let her go to see her daughter, to try to talk some sense into her. "Novitiate" indeed! Control. Mind control, just like they talked about on T.V.

Tomorrow she would make an appointment to talk with the Bishop again.

CHAPTER FOURTEEN

LIGHTENING UP

Althea, May 1975

If life is a journey, then Althea was a traveler who was always looking ahead to the next turning in the road, so she'd gotten pretty good at saying goodbye. The difference now was that the Brothers and Reverend Ursula had given her the sense that this wasn't the usual moving-on-but-will-be-back-to-visit kind of good-bye.

For one thing, she was allowed to bring with her only one suitcase. She was making a temporary vow of poverty for the next two and a half years, and was not allowed to own anything more. A couple of years earlier, when a friend's parents had sent her to Europe as their daughter's companion, she'd had a hard time fitting everything she thought she needed for those six weeks into two large suitcases. But joining the Holy Order of Mystical Evangelists was about letting go. Lightening up.

The first thing she arranged was a place to stash the box containing everything of consequence (at least of consequence to her) that she had ever written. Jana was great about taking it, and even borrowed Chad's car to drive up to Berkeley to pick it up. She didn't believe in God anymore but she believed in poetry, and she respected her friend for trying to write it. But she refused to come until after Althea had left.

"I don't understand," Althea said on the phone two weeks before she planned to leave. "Don't you have any time to say good-bye?"

"I don't have any desire to say good-bye," Jana answered.

"Are you angry with me?"

"No."

"Have I hurt your feelings?"

"Tricia, you wouldn't intentionally hurt my feelings."

Althea stifled the compulsion to correct her name. "Have I unintentionally hurt your feelings?"

Silence.

"Jana, I don't want for us to part like this."

Silence.

"Jana?"

"Yeah."

"You've been a really good friend."

"You too."

"A lot of times, you've been the only one who knew what was really going on with me, the only one who cared enough to find out."

Silence.

"You know I have to do this."

Silence. Still silence.

"Jana?" Althea could hear shrillness in her own voice.

"Exactly what is it you have to do, Tricia?"

"I have to find my way." Was that putting it in a way she could understand?

"You were finding your way just fine before, and it was you who was finding it."

"No. No, I wasn't. I was getting high. I was dating men I didn't love and who didn't love me. I felt desperate, and I was just thinking about myself. I was lost, Jana."

"And now, all of a sudden, you're found."

As with her mother, Althea knew she couldn't have this conversation yet again. Maybe Jana had a point about the suddenness of her decision, about natural, healthy growth happening gradually. How could she communicate the urgency she felt to go forward, to become something more? She couldn't let anything stop her, or anyone.

"Thank you for caring so much, Jana. I promise I'll write in three months, when I finish my novitiate and I'm able to have outside contact." It felt great to refer to her "novitiate" – so official, so respectable.

***

Getting rid of her other belongings should have been easy. After all, she'd arrived in Berkeley only a year and a half before with only a backpack containing a few articles of clothing, some toiletries, and a couple books. But now she had a nice acoustic guitar, a bicycle, a futon, a carved wooden trunk full of clothes, and a large shelf of books. All of these possessions meant something to her, not the least because, with her tiny income, she'd had to hunt, bargain, barter, or sacrifice for them. Every time she gave something away, she would stop to wonder whether in several months she might discover that she did not really have a calling, and have to start all over again to build a life in the world.

But sometimes it felt wonderful to give things away. Like giving the guitar to a street musician named Earl who always played outside Moe's Books and had had his guitar stolen. Or giving her gentle, soft-spoken friend, Elizabeth, the silver bracelet set with lapis lazuli with its bright blues and deep blues and flecks of white and gold that looked like the earth as seen from space. Once they'd hiked Mount Tamalpais together and descended to the beach to watch the sunset. She'd never forget it.

Althea was having coffee at the kitchen table one morning when Georgie surprised her by saying, "I wish I could be like you."

"You don't know me very well, or you wouldn't say that."

"I know you've got something. Class, maybe, but it's more than that. Maybe wisdom."

Althea laughed. "Oh, sure. Why don't you check with Father Todd on that one?"

"Okay, maybe not wisdom. Then deepness. Like a deep river."

"What a beautiful thing to say. But you've got depth, too, Georgie. Every person does. It's just hard to see sometimes, especially in ourselves."

"But I can see yours."

Then it occurred to her. "Georgie, what are you reading these days?"

"Reading? Nothing."

"Well, why not?"

"I don't know. I don't really read. I talk to people. Watch T.V."

"If you started reading good books, you could get to know more of what's inside you, and share it with other people."

Althea gave her the whole bookcase of titles, except for the Bible and T.S. Eliot.

Once she got started, giving things away was really freeing. One day she was walking down Shattuck Avenue on the way back from buying underwear and other necessities for the novitiate and student year. A woman passing smiled and said she liked her shoulder bag. It was an authentic Danish hunting bag made of caramel colored leather, a gift from people she'd stayed with on a visit to Denmark. That had been a lifetime ago when she was eighteen, before she'd met Jonathan, before she'd truly begun to build a life, and failed, and despaired, and wondered whether she would ever be able to hope again. Now here she was on a sunny spring morning, not only hoping, but anticipating a new beginning.

She slipped the bag from her shoulder, emptied the contents into her shopping bag, and extended her prized possession toward this stranger. "Take it, please, I don't need it anymore."

For the rest of her life, she kept a page from the journal she wrote during those last days before her novitiate with HOME. Oddly, she kept it with copies of early poems. Once a young woman, a fellow HOME student who also wrote poetry, was looking through her folder of poems. The woman stopped, surprised, and read it aloud:

To Do Before Leaving:

- Label boxes of poetry and make sure housemates know where they are when Jana comes for them
- Donate clothes to homeless shelter
- Write to say good-bye to Jonathan (I still love you but I won't tell you so again)
- Buy toothbrush and black tights
- Call my mother but don't tell her I'm scared

"This is a poem," the Sister had said.

Althea laughed. "It's a 'to-do' list."

"No, Sister Althea, it's a poem. I like it a lot better than the angst stuff or the idealistic stuff in most of your other pieces. It's so real."

"I guess it's as real as I knew how to be at the time," Althea said.

CHAPTER FIFTEEN

FAREWELLS

Althea, May 1975

"Prepare ye the way of the Lord, prepare ye the way of the Lord," chanted the voice from the record as Althea entered the room for the farewell party given her by Georgie and her other housemates. Several months before, they'd seen the film *Godspell* that opened with this song – a scene of young men and women leaving behind their old lives and plunging into a fountain to be baptized by a young, countercultural John the Baptist. The movie had seemed inspiring at the time, but now the song seemed to lack seriousness compared to what she was trying to do, to actually give her life to God. The world she was leaving behind, including this movie and even her friends' understanding of what she was about to do, was beginning to look shallow, and she was more certain daily that joining HOME was the right thing to do.

Over pizza and sodas, her friends quizzed her about what her new life would be like, and Althea struggled to respond in a way they would understand.

Starr said, "I lived in an ashram at Blue Mountain two years ago and it was far out. We worked and meditated and ate together, but everybody had to either have a job or have a lot of money saved up to buy what they needed. Is it like that?"

"It's maybe a little like that," Tricia said, not sure exactly what life in an ashram was like. "But we take a vow of poverty and everyone works and gives the money to the Brotherhood. That is, after the novitiate. Novices just work at the Brother house, not outside."

"It's more like being a nun, right?" said Isla, who had attended some of the classes at the Brother House.

"Yes, it's kind of like being a monk or a nun for the life vowed brothers and sisters, except they can get married and have families. But Father Todd says that for the first three months it's like being a baby in a whole new world. I'll mostly be taken care of and allowed to see how things are. That's why I won't be able to talk to anyone on the outside or write letters for three months. Then the next year is like being in a seminary, studying theology and working in an area of service. And of course going to all the chapel services."

"Whoa – a cemetery?" Barb said. Barb was high that night.

Georgie intervened. "Not cemetery, goofball, seminary – a school where people study about God."

"It sounds so *heavy*," Starr said. "At the ashram we could do what we wanted most of the time when we weren't meditating. Why would you want to take all that on?"

"Because she has a *calling*," Georgie interjected. "You have to be called to that kind of a life. I'm not – that's why I can't enter it."

A special calling, truly belonging. But what about Georgie? Why was she — Althea, who wasn't really very spiritual, specially called? Why wasn't there a place for Georgie in the Brotherhood, when she wanted so badly to join? Althea shoved this to the back of her mind along with the other unanswered questions.

As they finished eating and the excitement abated, she gave everyone a hug and left to get ready for the early morning departure. When she got to her room, though, there wasn't much of anything to get ready. Her "to-do" list was completed, her one suitcase was packed and standing by the door, and her room was empty except for a borrowed sleeping bag and a favorite outfit hanging in the closet ready for morning. She would have liked to telephone Jana one last time, but she knew that was potentially disastrous – Jana would either be silent and withdrawn or argue with her, and neither would be encouraging.

For the first time in a very long time she was alone with nothing to do, and it was unnerving. She alone would enter into this new life, except for the Lord, who felt very far away.

She opened the window to the gentle air of the May evening, leaned out, and looked up.

"Please go with me," she prayed. "I don't want to be alone."

There was no kind of answer she could perceive, and she went to sleep uneasy.

CHAPTER SIXTEEN

NAKED

Althea – May 1975

Althea woke at dawn, filled the claw-foot bathtub to the brim and plunged into what might be her last leisurely bath as a lay person. It was a good bath. The very hot water softened with lavender salts slid over her skin like silk. She was naked, not nude, she thought, a distinction the poet Graves wrote about. Nakedness was a body in unadorned simplicity, not slyly nude to impress someone or gain something. Her whole life was naked in that moment. She'd given away the props – the hippie clothes, the perfumed oils, the jewelry. She'd had a last, long phone conversation with her friend Luke in Buffalo during which he had impulsively, and so characteristically, asked her to marry him. To save her from herself? Then, in transparent relief that she'd refused, he'd told her he was proud that she was following her destiny.

Destiny – was that it? That sounded so self-important, something like Napoleon saying that a star of destiny told him to conquer the world. No, it wasn't destiny. It was a choice, a road, a simple path. There was a good reason for that cliché. The spiritual path. The path she was called to.

And she did hear a call, though of course that was also a metaphor. She didn't hear voices or see visions like some of the Brothers and Sisters said they did. This was probably a mercy, since she was no saint, and who knew where a vision might have come from – more likely from below than from above. But she had been trying to pray alone in her room, where it was really hard and where it really counted. In her room, she was apart from Brother Jarrell's supportive smile, apart from Father Todd's watchful eye, apart from a room full of others whose simple presence suggested that, yes, they all had found what they had been seeking and she had too.

In her room she had been trying to talk to God, and even to listen. She had been reading the Bible, reading over and over a passage from John 5 that her Bible fell open to nearly every time she picked it up:

...but I know you, that you do not have the love of
God in your heart. I have come in my Father's name,
and you do not accept me, but if someone else comes
in his own name, you will accept him.

She wasn't sure what this meant. She was terribly afraid that it meant she was depraved because she wanted so much for people to love her, because she wanted love so badly that she had been willing to make desperate choices that had alienated her from herself, from what she knew was good, and from God. All of this was surely true, but she had repented of it. Was she making the same mistake again – choosing people and their ideas over looking to God? But she was trying to look to God, and this Order was going to help her.

The decision was made now. She sank down into the water naked as the day she came into the world – ready to learn how to live in poverty, purity, humility, obedience, and service. Or so she believed.

PART TWO

NOVICE TRAINING

CHAPTER ONE

YOU WON'T BE NEEDING THIS

Althea – San Francisco, May 1975

A mockingbird sang outside the bedroom window and a cool breeze stirred the curtains. Althea dressed in a favorite outfit – drawstring pants of unbleached muslin and a hand-embroidered tunic of many colors on a black background. No make-up, of course, and her freshly washed hair pulled up into a simple twist the way the Sisters wore theirs. She took a deep breath, hoisted her big blue suitcase, gave a last look around the room where she had lived for a year and a half, and walked downstairs to the front door.

Georgie was waiting there for her, beaming. What a simple and kind woman she was.

"Your coach is waiting. Are you ready for your new life?"

"Let's hope so," she whispered. "You pray that I am, okay?"

Georgie nodded gravely, and they got into her red Volkswagen bug to drive across the Bay as the sun began to rise. It seemed all of Berkeley was in bloom with cherry and plum blossoms lining the streets and tulips and early roses in the gardens. Spring – a new beginning.

Georgie did her best to converse as they drove across the Bay Bridge and into San Francisco, but Althea had little to say. She studied the cloudless blue sky above and the sailboats dotting the blue water below. She breathed slowly, trying to calm herself. When they arrived at the HOME Center, Georgie leaned over to give her a hug.

"Aren't you coming in with me?"

Georgie smiled widely and shook her head. "No place for me here, Tricia. You go now, and follow your calling."

Hoisting her suitcase, she mounted the steep stairs. Reverend Ursula met her at the door, unsmiling but speaking kindly.

"Welcome to your novitiate, Althea. Come in for a moment while I find Sister Constance to help you get settled across the street."

Tricia looked around the comfortable parlor that the life-vowed Brothers and Sisters enjoyed, wondering when she might be able to sit in a sunny bay window to read one of the enticing books on the tall shelves that lined the room.

Reverend Ursula did not return, but after a few moments a short, pert blonde woman in a black dress and clerical collar appeared in the doorway.

"Althea? You can follow me," she said without introduction.

They crossed the street as birds sang in the adjacent park and the sun warmed her shoulders. She followed Sister Constance up the narrow stairs of the Novice House to a small bedroom painted blue, with a high ceiling and an oriental carpet in blues and browns. A set of bunk beds was set against each of two walls, with a large chest of drawers against a third and tall windows of lovely old glass occupying the fourth.

"You'll share this room with three other women. The beds to the right are taken, but the fourth novice hasn't arrived yet, so you get to pick either the top or bottom of the bed on the left."

"Okay. I pick the top. I might fall off, but at least I won't feel claustrophobic," Althea said, grinning, in an attempt at friendly conversation.

Sister Constance ignored her remark, walked to the chest, and began opening drawers. "The two bottom ones are empty, so you can pick one."

"Thank you." In an effort to practice humility, Tricia resolved to take the very bottom drawer but not to say anything about it. That seemed like something a disciple ought to do.

Sister Constance showed her the bathroom that joined this bedroom to another similar one. It had another window of lovely old glass over a large sink.

"We will provide you with shampoo, soap, toothpaste, and deodorant. If you have any other toiletries, you can put them on that shelf," she said, indicating a single wooden shelf with several bottles of hand lotion and face cream. "Whatever you put there is shared by everyone, though. You can keep your toothbrush and anything else private in your drawer."

That sounded messy and potentially unsanitary, but Althea didn't say anything. Maybe she could use the top of the dresser for a few things; that would be at least semi-private. Who would use someone else's toothbrush?

Sister Constance disappeared through the door of the closet and called in a muffled voice, "What's your dress size?"

"Uh, small." Then she remembered the granola bingeing and the fact that recently her dresses had been fairly shapeless. "Or maybe medium."

She stuck out her head and frowned. "Medium, like a size ten?"

Her cheeks grew hot. "I used to be a size six, but I've gained some weight in the last couple of months."

Sister Constance looked her over appraisingly. "Let's try a ten and a twelve."

Althea wanted to cry. This was a moment she had been anticipating for months – receiving her black garb – but now she was ashamed to have put so much weight onto her small frame. Was gluttony her main sin, she wondered, or the fear that prompted it? In any case, overeating wasn't something a disciple would do. She promised herself to eat sparingly during her novitiate to atone.

Sister Constance reappeared with two black dresses cut exactly like her own. The difference between the garb of a novice and the garb of a Sister, whether student or life-vowed, was that a Sister wore a collar and a cross.

"Go ahead and try them on," she said, and to Althea's dismay she remained standing there as if Althea were a child she was dressing. Glad she'd worn a tee shirt underneath, she removed her tunic, slipped the smaller of the two dresses over her head, and tugged it over her body before removing her muslin pants. The dress was snug, but it would work, especially when she was alone and could remove the tee shirt. She was not going to accept the larger size.

Sister Constance picked up Tricia's favorite tunic and looked at it admiringly.

Althea smiled. "It's hand-embroidered in India. It was a gift from my friend Daphne."

"Is that Daphne who's a novice with us now?"

Tricia nodded.

"Well, she probably gave it to you because she knew she wouldn't need it here. It won't be until next fall that you novices will take your student vows and be assigned to centers for your year of student training. Then you'll need clothes to wear to whatever job you have in the world, but not until then. And anyway, the Sisters share all their clothes." She draped Althea's many-colored tunic over her arm. "You won't be needing this."

Althea wanted to object. She wanted to tell this cold and grabby person that she didn't have any right to take her clothes. But if she said that, she would be wrong. She had given her – had given them – the right.

"I'll leave you to unpack now. Lunch will be at noon in the novice's dining room downstairs." She nodded and walked out the door. To Althea's recollection, Sister Constance never spoke a word to her again during the three months she lived across the street from her, though on a Saturday afternoon not long afterward, Althea saw her walking down the sidewalk in the embroidered tunic, and couldn't help smiling when she saw that it was too way too big for her.

CHAPTER TWO

THIS NEW NOVICE

Reverend Ursula – San Francisco, May 1975

As Novice Master, Reverend Ursula had guided dozens of raw beginners through their three-month training. Some were naturals, in touch with their spiritual natures, aware of the great privilege of being part of one of the foremost centers for spiritual training in the country, humbled at the thought of cooperating with Divine revelation, immediately obedient and teachable.

Then there were those like this new novice, Patricia, now Althea. Why had she been given such an exalted name? She was already full of herself. At her very first visit she had asked dozens of questions, mostly about what kinds of liberties she could retain as a novice. A person would think that she was being deprived instead of being given a priceless gift. When could she use the library? What about letters to friends and family? What – no outside contact for three months? If she didn't complain in words, her facial expressions communicated clearly enough. Evidently this undisciplined young woman had little to no understanding of what a novitiate is.

Now, a month later, she had arrived and was ready to begin, and how she would do remained to be seen. She had seemed sincere enough when Reverend Ursula met her at the door this morning. At least she had obeyed and brought only one suitcase, although it was a large one. It was probably filled with books that would need to be examined for appropriateness and no doubt stored for her until she took her temporary vows in three months and began her student year, but even for a student some of her books were bound to be disallowed. Father Todd had said she was some kind of poet living in Berkeley, though he hadn't read her poems. Reverend Ursula could only imagine.

Still, she had come, relatively free from physical baggage, and expressing the desire to grow and change. She deserved just as much attention and care as any of the others, and Reverend Ursula was committed to giving it to her.

Now, in the novice chapel, she led through the brief prayer service the young woman kneeling before her and witnessed her vow of obedience, the only vow required of a novice.

"Althea, traveler on life's journey, do you promise to obey your spiritual directors in all good things, and to cooperate with them without complaint or resistance, so that you may begin to answer to the High Calling?"

"I do promise to obey my spiritual directors in all good things and to cooperate with them in answering the High Calling."

"Rise Novice Althea of the Holy Order of Mystical Evangelists."

Reverend Ursula extended her hand, palm up, and Althea placed in it her right hand. A gesture of help on the part of the Novice Master, a gesture of trust on the part of the novice.

CHAPTER THREE

Two Days and Two Nights

Novice Althea – May 1975

One of the first initiations for a novice was a period of fasting, silence, and meditation in the chapel. Like the anticipated vows of poverty, purity, humility, obedience, and service, this practice was borrowed from western monasticism.

As she dressed that morning, Althea considered the vow of obedience she had taken the night before. It was supposed to be the simplest vow, yet it frightened her more than the others. She knew a little about voluntary poverty, or at least voluntary simplicity, and she looked forward to it. She understood the nobility of the vow of purity, and she knew that it was good. Humility? Eh, very difficult for her, but not scary, because it was kind of exalted and hard to measure. Service, absolutely – doing good work was part of leading a good life. But "obedience to spiritual directors"? She didn't know any of these people. How could she trust them?

Immediately after evening prayers last night, Reverend Ursula had sent her to her room for the 9 p.m. curfew, instructing Althea to rise and dress at five-thirty a.m., go to the novice chapel for 6 a.m. morning prayers, and meet her immediately afterward in the hallway of the novice house, since she would not be eating break-fast. Novice Althea had obeyed in every detail. She had met two of her three roommates and spoken with them briefly before lights out. One was a very short and slightly built brunette from Texas who spoke quietly and seldom. The other was a tall and dignified young Black woman who described herself as the daughter of an African Methodist Episcopal minister, and whose manners were formal, impeccable, and kind. Neither tempted her to talk past lights out, and to her surprise she fell asleep a little after laying her head on the pillow, in spite of the new surroundings.

Now this morning she stood in the hallway, waiting. Her empty stomach growling as the delicious smell of coffee, toast, and butter wafted towards her. Worse yet was the bacon cooking. She had been a vegetarian for the past year but when she had mentioned that last night at dinner, Reverend Ursula passed her a plate of roasted chicken, telling her that novices work hard and need to eat meat, and that no one in HOME is a vegetarian unless specif-ically directed to be. So obedience began. Althea put a piece of chicken on her plate, cut a piece, took a deep breath, and slowly put it in her mouth while all the other novices watched her. She knew she needed to smile and nod, but she found she didn't have to force herself; it was delicious, and this morning the bacon smelled delicious.

Now Reverend Ursula approached Althea, laying her finger on her lips to remind the novice not to speak. The sky was just begin-ning to lighten as she followed the Novice Master across the street to the main house, down the stone steps of the garden, and into the cool, tomb-like darkness of the main chapel. This chapel was long and narrow, with an altar against the farthest wall, much like an old-style Catholic or Episcopal church. Since the room had pre-viously been a basement, the ceiling was quite low and the small windows set high in one of the walls let in very little light. The floor was covered with a deep red carpet and folding chairs were set out in rows facing the altar, while in the back was an open space with a shrine to Mary in the corner, which was the only image in the room. A large wooden cross was suspended over the altar. Other than that, the chapel was unadorned. Where was the image of Jesus?

"You understand what is expected," Reverend Ursula said in a quiet, firm voice. "You will remain here today and tonight without speaking to anyone. Use the time for prayer, self-reflection, and meditation. Practice meditating to seek the Light. There is a Bible on the back shelf if you wish to read it. You have a pitcher of water and a glass on the back shelf as well, and the lavatory is through that door over there. Try to forget hunger, to forget your body entirely. Focus on the spirit. Tomorrow, one of the sisters will bring you a small meal of fruit and nuts to lighten your fast, but you will continue to speak to no one, and to spend tomorrow as well in prayer, self-reflection, and meditation. On the second morning, all the brothers, sisters, and novices will join you here for the Sunday service, and you will break your fast with the other novices afterward. This is a rare opportunity for stillness. Use it wisely."

Novice Althea had a hundred questions, but she couldn't speak, so she nodded, and Reverend Ursula left her. Left her alone. Reverend Ursula wasn't the most comforting of presences Althea had known, but she was one of only a few familiar faces in this new world.

After a moment, Althea walked toward the altar, knelt, and prayed the Our Father. Then she just spoke to God for a while, explaining that she was frightened and lonely and unsure of what she was supposed to be doing. That took about ten minutes or so. After that, she sat on one of the folding chairs to face the fact that she was going to have to be alone with herself for two days and two nights.

Being alone in silence for an hour would be a terrific challenge for most people, particularly if they were not reading or writing, but were just sitting still. "Be still and know that I am God," said the psalm, but to hear this and to do it were entirely different. Althea had always been very, very uncomfortable being alone without something to occupy her mind. No, not just uncomfortable, but ready to crawl out of her own skin.

Of course, being in this situation was her own doing and she knew it. Since entering adulthood, she had not been living a godly life, and her heart was full of thoughts and memories that could not stand in the light, let alone the Light, whatever that was.

Now she was alone. Alone, scared, and still somewhat lost and uncertain. Alone with all the cruddy things she had done and thought for twenty-one years. Alone with God, not necessarily because God was especially in this chapel and she was trying to be a spiritual novice, but simply because she was sitting still and God was everywhere inside and outside of her. The pressure was unbearable.

She took the Bible and began to read Genesis, to begin at the beginning, but after Chapter One she couldn't concentrate anymore. She closed her eyes and breathed as she had learned to do some time ago, hoping to find the Spirit, but obviously she was not worthy, because she found no peace. Though she didn't have a clock, she guessed that about two hours total had gone by, with at least forty-six hours left. She paced the long, narrow room, desperate. Would everyone find out that she was no spiritual person at all, but a horrible person with a dark heart, a miserable fake, probably hopeless?

She said the Our Father again. She talked to God again and told Him she was desperate, and horrible, and a fake, and probably hopeless. Then she did the only thing she could think of to do – she lay down on the floor while it was still only mid-morning, and went to sleep.

When she woke the windows were dark and the votive candle burning on the altar lit the room dimly. Her mouth felt like the inside of a garbage can, her stomach ached, and she became acutely aware that she hadn't eaten anything since last night's dinner. It was not only silence and solitude that were foreign to her – she had never fasted this long or this hard before, but only kept the regular Catholic fasts before she stopped being Catholic. In the world of ascetic fasting, she was a total lightweight. She headed for the water pitcher and filled her stomach with water, which helped for a little while with both the horrible taste in her mouth and the gnawing in her stomach.

For the remainder of that very long night, Althea alternated between trying to pray, trying to read Scripture, and lying on the carpet waiting for morning. If she had harbored any ideas that she was now a spiritual warrior, that night banished them. The struggles she would wage with her fallen, wounded self loomed large before her, and she felt neither armed or brave. It was almost unbearable not to be busy, not to be distracted. She lay down and fell asleep again, until she was wakened by a knock on the chapel door.

Grabbing a quick drink of water to purge her nasty breath (why had she not brought a toothbrush and toothpaste to this long weekend?), Althea opened the door to a tall woman garbed in the knee-length black dress, cross, and collar of a life-vowed sister.

"Good morning, Althea. I'm Sister Lois, the cook. I imagine you must be pretty hungry. Don't answer, though – remember the silence." Her brown eyes smiled kindly, and she was carrying a tray of foods that looked as if they had been gathered from the Garden of Eden. Half a cantaloupe filled with creamy yoghurt. Blackberries and strawberries. A bowl of walnuts. A steaming teapot. Althea's mouth watered as she examined the feast.

Sister Lois laughed. "Most novices aren't used to fasting on water."

Althea raised her eyebrows and nodded.

"You'll need to break the fast slowly. I recommend just eating the yoghurt first, and waiting a bit for the fruit and nuts."

Althea nodded and followed Sister Lois into the early sunlight of the garden, where she set the tray on a small wrought-iron table next to a bush of fragrant yellow roses, pulled up a chair for Althea, and smiled. In the sunlight, Althea saw that this Sister had caramel-colored skin and dark brown hair – a warm-looking woman with a warm demeanor.

"Can I get you anything else?"

Althea nodded, and mimed brushing her teeth with her finger.

She laughed. "You wouldn't be the first to forget a toothbrush and toothpaste. I'll be back in a few minutes. But first, let's pray."

She turned east to the sun, lifted her hands, closed her eyes, and asked a blessing on Althea's food. Althea studied her strong, tan hands and was thankful that they had prepared this meal.

When Sister Lois left, Althea ate some of the yoghurt slowly. She had never tasted plain yoghurt before; it was tart, a little sour, but creamy and rich. She nibbled one blackberry and then another for sweetness, and drank a cup of the peppermint tea. Remembering Sister Lois's words and wanting to please this new friend, she stopped at that, and was smelling the roses when Sister Lois returned, toothbrush and toothpaste in hand.

"Those are Peace Roses," she said. "Aren't they lovely? Did you know that yellow roses symbolize friendship?"

Althea smiled and shook her head.

"I've been reading a book about Victorian flower symbols. Red roses are for love, pink are for innocence, white are for purity. I planted all these roses last year after I took my life vows." Her face beamed. "I'll tell you something even more wonderful – want to hear it?"

Althea nodded enthusiastically.

"Ivy is for Faith. Hawthorne sprigs are for Hope. Roses are for Love. The three great virtues, Althea – Faith, Hope, and Love."

Althea smiled her gratitude. Maybe she could look forward to reading that beautiful book about Victorian flower symbols. Maybe

Sister Lois, her new friend, would lend it to her. If she could just get through the next three months. Yellow roses for friendship. She broke off a small bud and extended it to Sister Lois, who put her arm around Althea's shoulders.

"God bless you, Althea."

Althea watched as Sister Lois walked off to leave her to her second day and night.

*****

After bringing the rest of the food inside and brushing her teeth, Althea sat on the floor facing the large wooden cross that hung above the altar. What now? She inhaled deeply and exhaled slowly several times. Breath and Spirit, the same word, as she had learned in her confused and difficult self-study of comparative religions while in Buffalo. The intellectual search without a spiritual foundation had contributed to a deep depression, along with the diet pills and sleeplessness that had accompanied it. The ordeal had taught her that she couldn't find God with her mind or even with her own will, no matter how hard she tried, though she had to try, and try with all her will. This was why she needed the Order, needed help and wisdom from people who knew God better than she did. It couldn't be the Catholic Church anymore, though it had to be a Christian faith, and she couldn't see any reason why a Protestant church would be significantly better than the Catholic church had been. "Churchianity," Father Todd had called the practice of established churches – more emphasis on institutions and rules than on faith and love. Jesus had revealed a better way to Great Master Peter and he had passed it down through the Master Teachers, the Self-Realized Ones, Father Todd explained.

She had experienced Baptism, the first initiation. Now she had to seek the Light, find it inside herself so that she could receive Illumination. But first she needed to be cleansed, and in a big way.

She sighed, breathed again, closed her eyes and saw – a negative image against darkness of the cross she had been staring at. Was this a vision? Nah, because she also saw an image of the altar and the rows of chairs. It was what anyone would see after staring at something in semi-darkness.

She sat for what seemed a very long time with eyes closed, seeing nothing of any significance and feeling the food and warm tea in her stomach. Body and spirit – she was both, but a lot more aware of body than spirit, and feeling very sleepy now. Though it was probably no later than ten in the morning, she lay down on the sleeping bag and drifted away.

When she woke she could still see light through the high windows of the basement chapel. Still Saturday, still alone in this place trying to become holy. Dear God.

She splashed her face in the small lavatory sink, brushed her teeth again, and drank two big glasses of water. Then she remembered the remaining fruit and nuts, and devoured every bit.

What next? She could read the Bible while it was still light. She went out into the garden, now growing a little cool in the early evening, and opened to Psalms. She had always liked reading these holy poems of King David, especially in the beautiful King James translation, and now she paged through them to see which opening verse would speak to her heart. Ah, here – Psalm 51. "Have mercy on me, O God, according to Thy great mercy…." Mercy, from *merci* in French, she remembered – a gift, a grace, not something she had earned but something given out of the goodness of the giver. Of the Giver. No wonder she hadn't been able to find the light. How could she find it on her own, or how could anyone? It was a gift. She read on: "Thou shalt wash me, and I shall be made whiter than snow….Create in me a clean heart, O God, and renew a right spirit within me."

When Althea closed her eyes now, it wasn't to try to hunt out The Light. "Have mercy on me, O God, according to Thy great mercy" she prayed, and breathed, and prayed and breathed, until the sun dipped below the horizon and she realized she was shivering. Back in the warm chapel, she wrapped up in the sleeping bag and remembered how the evening prayer called Vespers was actually the beginning of the new day. This was now the ending of her initiation, slowly becoming the beginning of her novitiate. Lying down, she prayed and breathed some more until she fell back asleep.

At last, light appeared at the high windows of the basement chapel, and she freshened up for the Sunday service. As the light brightened, Brothers and Sisters began to arrive, first those who were caring for the altar, then those who wanted quiet time before the service, and eventually everyone including the novices, who were led by Reverend Ursula to the front row of folding chairs. Althea caught the eye of her Novice Master, who motioned her to a chair.

Her first Sunday service as a novice was similar to those she had attended at the Brother House, but grander, with three priests serving and a full choir of the assembled Brothers, Sisters, and novices.

When the first rows of novices arose to commune, Althea took a deep breath and stood as straight as she could. She was a novice in the Holy Order of Mystical Evangelists, and she was about to receive the Body and Blood of the Master, to be changed into a being of Light.

Returning to her seat, Althea sang the thanksgiving hymns with all her heart. She emerged from the chapel and crossed the street in the glorious morning sunshine, believing that she was renewed.

CHAPTER FOUR

AN ORDERLY LIFE?

Novice Althea – Spring 1975

One of the first things Althea noticed about life in HOME was the beauty – even artistry – of the environment. Both the Victorian house the novices occupied and the one across the street where the life-vowed members made their home were graciously designed and appointed with rich wooden floors and trim, high ceilings with plaster ornaments and crystal chandeliers, and antique furniture. Even more than that, what impressed itself vividly on Althea was the way the magnificent San Francisco light – bright and moisture-laden – streamed through the fine original glass windows. The window over the sink in the bathroom she used faced east, and in the morning she felt she was washing herself not only with water but with sunlight.

There was also an ascetic beauty to the way the novices dressed – the simple black dresses and shoes, the absence of jewelry or make-up, the stern upswept hairdos. She felt unmasked in a way she liked – her basic self, at least if she were to overlook the layers of pretense even she was aware of in her personality, or to hope that in time she would put aside these, too.

Their schedule was rigorous, rising at six a.m. to dress, arriving to the chapel by six-thirty for the morning service. On all days but Sunday, services were held in their own chapel in the basement of the novice quarters, with Reverend Ursula officiating.

After services, they had breakfast in the dining room of the novice house. The food was plentiful, healthful, and delicious, including yoghurt, bacon, eggs, toast or oatmeal, fresh fruit, and coffee. It occurred to Althea, who had been supporting herself for years, that someone was paying for her to eat well for these three months. Were her benefactors convinced of the holiness of their mission, or relying on getting some return from her? Or both?

It was easier than she'd expected to abandon the vegetarian diet she'd been following since arriving in California a year and a half before, and to obediently eat the omnivorous diet set before her. Though she half-heartedly debated with some other novices that avoiding meat was both healthy and spiritually productive, Reverend Ursula's word had been law at that first evening's dinner and was ever after. Just eat what you're given, in obedience and humility. Althea didn't notice any negative effects beyond a couple of days when she felt overly full, even if the blow to her pride was painful.

Once the breakfast dishes were finished, the novices went to their assigned work. Althea's duties on Mondays, Wednesdays, and Fridays included cleaning at the main house: dusting, sweeping, vacuuming, and washing floors in the common areas. Her favorite room to clean was the sitting room, with its floor to ceiling book-shelves that she scanned at every opportunity, and its bay window through which the golden light poured on a sunny morning. Once there was a vase of deep red peonies, possibly the loveliest flowers she had ever seen, in honor of the birthday of one of the priests. She stroked their silky petals and inhaled their heady fragrance, wondering what it would be like to be able to afford to buy flowers like these.

Many of the life-vowed residents were really messy. Although cigarettes were banned, many sisters as well as brothers smoked pipes, which were considered more civilized. She could understand that the fresh smoke from cured pipe tobacco was preferable to the chemical smell of cigarettes, but the ashes still stank, and they were everywhere. So were the newspapers, books, empty coffee cups, and abandoned personal items such as reading glasses that she had to clear away before she could begin to clean. Worst of all was the bathroom used by some of the life-vowed sisters whose duties concluded about the same time hers should have done, and who regularly showered shortly before the noon deadline for completing her work and reporting to the Novice Quarters for lunch. They were getting ready for noon lunch too, leaving the floor a pasty mix of hair, water, and talcum powder that clung to the baseboards, corners, and tile grouting, defying her to remove it. To rub salt – or talcum powder – into her wounds, the same fluffed and buffed sisters would breeze past her every day while she crawled around on her hands and knees panicking about finishing before lunch, even though she would have to skip showering.

One day as she knelt on the threshold of this bathroom, rushing to finish, she felt a reassuring hand on her shoulder and looked up into the smiling face of one of the Master Teachers, Master Aphrodite-Maria, whom she had seen before only in photographs. She was very tall, maybe close to six feet, or so it seemed, with rose-gold hair, ivory skin, and kind, smiling green eyes. She was ten or more years older than Althea, in the prime of her thirties, dressed in a long white robe trimmed in gold, and she did indeed appear to be a goddess.

"Bless you, little one. You are offering good work, and this time of trial will be over shortly."

Althea was speechless as the Master Teacher floated away down the hall.

After that encounter, Althea threw herself into the work with great zeal. This was how she was serving God, and it needed to be the best that she could give. A few weeks later, Reverend Ursula came to check on her because she was taking longer than expected to complete her cleaning. She watched her for a moment, and then laughed.

"Sister Althea, no wonder it's taking you so long. You have so much resistance! You're pushing the broom with half your energy, and pulling it back with the other half. Try dancing with the broom, like this."

Reverend Ursula really did dance with that broom, as lightly and gracefully as a ballerina, and she thoroughly swept the rest of the floor in just a couple of moments. Smiling, she returned the broom to Althea, who realized that she had never seen her Novice Master smile before. Her softened face was pretty in its own way, not just formidable.

"Do you see the difference?"

"Yes, thank you."

"Don't be long, now. Lunch is served," she added as she left.

Althea tried to dance with the mop as she finished up her duties. Maybe it had something to do with not being afraid to fail?

On Tuesdays, she was assigned to the laundry room, a long, narrow space located at the back of the novice quarters. This was indeed a busy place, where the clothing and linens of about seventy-five people were kept clean. The system was ingenious. Each person labelled his or her clothing, either with laundry markers or, for those with the foresight, with woven labels sewn into the garments. Every Tuesday, they bundled all their soiled clothing into a pillow case and brought it to the laundry room along with the week's sheets and towels. The men pinned their socks together, and the women tied their tights in a knot with the feet and top loose. On Tuesday evenings, their clean, folded laundry was set on their beds, along with fresh sheets and towels.

Althea enjoyed working in the damp, warm laundry room in the cool mornings of the San Francisco summer when the fog lingered late. The occasional warm, sunny mornings presented a challenge, but the door and windows were opened to catch a cooling breeze from the Bay. Something about the clean smell of the detergent and the process of piling the fresh laundry in neat stacks was very fulfilling. It was good to do something useful and not to have to think too much.

Less enjoyable was her Thursday morning kitchen duty, not with loveable Sister Lois, but with her assistant, Sister Pamela. Althea enjoyed preparing food, and in fact had worked in a number of restaurants in the past several years, but this recently life-vowed Sister was never happy to see her. Sister Pamela was a simple woman from somewhere in the Midwest, solidly built, hard-working, and brusque in her way of speaking. She also had very strong ideas about how things should be, and she did not like to have them challenged. Althea discovered this her first day on lunch duty when she was scrubbing vegetables to chop.

"What in the world are you doing washing those green onions?"

"Oh, just getting the soil off of them, and any pesticides that –"

"Well stop it. I can't stand to see you do that. It makes me sick."

Althea took a deep breath. By this time, she had realized that she should save any questions addressed to a person with more authority than she had – which would be nearly everyone – for those times when she truly needed an answer.

"How would you like for me to prepare them?" she said, hoping she sounded humble and helpful.

"Just cut off the roots, peel off anything wilted, and chop them. And from now on don't wash any of the vegetables."

Althea did as she was told. It was not about being right; it was about being obedient. A little dirt wouldn't hurt anybody, and hopefully a little pesticide wouldn't either.

Morning duties concluded with lunch, dishes, and a class taught by Reverend Ursula. Sometimes class would be on a selection from Scripture as Reverend Ursula interpreted it, sometimes on the teachings of HOOM as revealed to its founder, Father Peter, and sometimes on theological writings such as those of Dionysius the Aereopagite or literary works with spiritual themes, such as Tennyson's *Idylls of the King*. This last annoyed and distressed Althea because she could not believe that literal, pragmatic Reverend Ursula understood poetry anywhere nearly as well as did she herself. After all, Althea had studied and written literature all her life, even if that life amounted to only a little more than twenty years. She dreamed of the day she would be able to teach the beauty of literature.

"Althea, take that far-away expression off your face and simply pay attention to the class," Reverend Ursula said.

"Sorry. I was just listening to music of the rhythm."

"Oh, were you? And what would you know about poetic rhythms?"

Althea sighed, knowing she must not answer that question. Reverend Ursula was trying to teach her humility. She hoped that, with her high spiritual attainment, the Novice Master was not able to read her mind.

I am a straight A English major, a published poet, a freaking artist, Althea's mind screamed. *You don't know me, you can't see me, you don't love me, no one knows me, no one sees me, no one loves me.*

Silent tears stung her eyes, but she breathed deeply to stop them. She didn't say a word.

CHAPTER FIVE

THIS NEW NOVICE, AGAIN

Reverend Ursula – June 1975

Reverend Ursula sighed as she exited the altar on Sunday night after evening prayers and made her way down the long, narrow hallway, where any of her charges might approach needing anything, en route to the stairs and the haven of her private quarters. It had been a very long day, though it was supposed to be a day of rest.

First thing in the morning, well before the 10 a.m. service, the parents of one of the novices had arrived with handlers from a rescue group, demanding to see their son and bring him home. The policy in that case was always to allow a visit. After all, the Holy Order of Mystical Evangelists was not a cult though it was so often accused of being one, she reminded the Brother on door duty. They had nothing to hide. The young male novice was escorted to the sitting room of the main house, where his parents found him nicely clothed, fed, and insisting that he wanted to stay. This sort of encounter was one of the hardest parts of her role as Novice Master, and she had bitten her tongue many times during the interview, since it was her duty simply to remain present to support the novice and prevent any use of force. The mother cried, the father yelled, and the handler, evidently a psychologist, advised and attempted to persuade, but the young man remained adamant. It was over an hour before the visitors left, vowing to return to "rescue" their son. To rescue their son from his spiritual calling. It had been no fit preparation for the service.

Now she could hear commotion behind her and turned around.

"Reverend Ursula, Reverend Ursula!" It was Althea, of course, pushing through the hall past the other novices. Althea, who seemed to live in a state of crisis.

"Reverend Ursula!" she cried again, only a foot away.

"Child, you do not need to shout. What could be the matter?"

"Could I talk with you please, about something really important?"

"It's late, Althea. Can't it wait until tomorrow after lunch?"

Althea's large green eyes were wide and a bit wild.

"That's such a long time. Please."

"Very well," she answered, steering the novice into a small reception room and gesturing toward a chair. "What is the matter?"

Althea perched on the edge of the chair and locked eyes with Reverend Ursula. "I can't meditate. I know I'm supposed to meditate twice a day so I can receive Illumination, but I can't do it."

"What do mean, you can't do it? You simply sit still, close your eyes, and focus on your solar plexus. We had an entire class on this during your first week."

Tears streamed down Althea's face. This was a very highly strung young woman, and one who thought a lot, in fact, too much. Certainly too much for a novice.

"Yes, yes, I remember, and I've been doing what you said, but I don't see The Light. I don't see visions. I'm just too earthy and dense."

"What do you see?"

"Just stuff. Images of what I was looking at before I closed my eyes, like a candle flame or somebody's face. Or a memory sometimes, like places I've been or people's faces."

"Well, some people have more resistance than others, but it isn't hopeless. You came here because you want Self-realization, didn't you?"

Althea was silent for a long moment while Reverend Ursula studied her face. Maybe this young woman didn't come to their Holy Order to become Self-realized. Maybe she was just lonely and wanted to belong to something – it had happened before – but why not join a choir or a club? Why take on so much discipline?

"Not really," she said, finally. "I came because I need to find God, and it seemed like God wanted me here because He sent Brother Jarrell to find me and bring me to class and then Father Todd answered questions I didn't even know how to ask. So I came here. Because I don't want to die after living some stupid, useless life. I want my life to mean something important. I came because I want to really live – forever."

Now the child was sobbing, bent over, her face in her hands. Reverend Ursula brought her a box of tissues from a nearby table, and drew her own chair closer. She put her hand on the novice's shoulder and waited for the tears to subside.

When Althea raised her head, wiped her eyes, blew her nose, and breathed deeply several times, Reverend Ursula spoke again.

"Althea, do you know that your name, the name that came down from above at your Baptism, means 'healing'?

She nodded.

"You need healing, Althea, and that could take a long time. You aren't a spiritual person right now, but you want to be, don't you?"

"Yes."

"Good. Healing and cleansing can take a long time, so you'll have to be patient. You have come to the foremost spiritual school in the country, and it is a privilege to be here. Do you understand that?"

Although the novice nodded, she did not look convinced. And why would she, since she was not looking for a spiritual school, but for salvation, and she wasn't connecting the two.

"Can you try to be obedient and patient, and see what happens?"

"Yes, I'll try."

Reverend Ursula sat for long moments after Althea had left, asking the Master to show her what in the world to do with this new novice.

CHAPTER SIX

SUFI DANCING?

July 1975 – Althea

Reverend Ursula's friend, a Sufi dance master named Danah, had visited the Novice Quarters several times. The petite, smiling woman in flowing dress was a perfect foil to the Novice Master, and fascinated Althea. Her fascination turned to anxiety, though, when she learned that at the next Saturday outing Danah would lead the novices in Sufi Dancing.

Until now, the focus of the classes and services she had attended had been on Christian principles found in the Bible. She had been delighted to see how these truths were often expressed in other religions, but she had never expected to be personally involved in other religious practices. Now it was required.

Graceful Danah seemed to dance even as she moved from one novice to another, crowning the women with wreaths of jasmine and the men with wreaths of ivy. Althea's sinuses pounded with the heady perfume of the flowers and she had to remove the wreath, explaining to an irked Reverend Ursula about her allergies and asthma.

The dancing itself was beautiful, with the smiling, laughing dance master leading them in a circle, chanting in the warm spring sunshine. But what was she chanting? It was in another language, probably Arabic. Althea resolved not even to hum along with the music. Those words meant something, were confessing something, and no one had asked her whether it was something she could confess.

After evening prayers that night she asked to speak with Reverend Ursula, who sighed loudly.

"Althea, again? What is it now?"

"The Sufi dancing. I didn't feel right participating."

The Novice Master's usually even tone broke. She seized Althea by the wrist and answered in an angry voice, "Child, you need to understand that a novice is like the Fool in the Tarot deck, stepping out in blind faith and obedience."

"I do understand, Reverend Ursula. Father Todd taught me about the need for humility and obedience. He showed me the Fool card and told me that Fool was me, stepping off a cliff with faith. I do have faith in the Master and I really don't know much of anything, but the fear of the Lord is the beginning of wisdom and my heart is telling me that a Christian person shouldn't be Sufi dancing and chanting whatever it was you were all chanting today."

Reverend Ursula's eyes blazed, belying her measured speech. "You are a novice. You have been with The Holy Order of Mystical Evangelists for all of eight weeks. You are not to quote Scripture to a Self-realized priest."

"Oh, I'm sorry, Reverend Ursula. I didn't mean to insult you, really, and I want to be obedient but it just didn't feel right. I mean, I am a Christian, not a Sufi, not a Muslim. What was she singing? What did it mean?"

"I do not know what the words of our sister Danah's song meant, but I do know that she was using them to praise God. The mission of The Holy Order of Mystical Evangelists is "Uniting

All Faiths." This is what the Master of Masters, Jesus, revealed to Father Paul. The New Age will not be about separate religions, but about all who seek God knowing Him through the Spiritual Path of Baptism, Illumination, and Self-realization. This is the Path that Jesus Our Master walked, that the Master Teachers are walking, and that you, novice Althea, have set your foot upon. It will be a New Age of Enlightenment, and HOME is established to help bring it about, so it is natural that its Brothers, Sisters, and Priests know the tenets of all major religions and show how they are one. It is natural and necessary to form relationships with people in all religions. I do not need to explain my decision to you, but since you are so concerned – suddenly – about spiritual purity, this is why I brought you to the Sufi dancing."

Reverend Ursula was sure and forceful, and her anger shook Althea to the core. She apologized again for giving offense, but not for objecting to the Sufi dancing. She could easily believe that she herself did not understand such high matters, especially direct revelation from God, but she also believed that she was in charge of her own life, her own soul, and she was still perplexed. All religions coming together – surely someone had misunderstood the revelation. Maybe all the Christian sects would come together eventually – that made sense and if it were possible it would be wonderful. She understood – had realized years ago – that God had revealed Himself to people all over the world before the birth of Christ and they had reached toward Him as toward the sun. Jews, of course, and Babylonians who worshipped Ahura Mazda as One God, and the Egyptians who were martyred for their faith in One God, Aten, and Native Americans who knew the Great Spirit. Then God became a human being and more fully revealed Himself. It was and ever would be Him that she worshipped – One God in Trinity, Father, Son, and Holy Spirit.

Reverend Ursula was cuttingly sarcastic when she said Althea was "suddenly concerned with spiritual purity," but she either couldn't or wouldn't understand. She meant, of course, that as Tricia, Althea had led a very unspiritual life, wanting the world desperately, and not doing much of anything for her soul. Althea surely wasn't proud of some of those worldly choices, but they were a far cry from committing blasphemy or heresy by false worship. To respect the worship of others who believed differently, to recognize their sincerity, was not the same as to worship with them and so affirm all that they believed. She knew she would never go again, no matter the consequences.

Yet the mission statement of HOME said, "We acknowledge Christ Jesus as the Lord of Earth and the spiritual head of our Order." That was clear. And in HOME she was being given a way to pray to God and serve God, a structure for a whole life which she hadn't been able to find anywhere else in the past years of searching. Though the image of Christ was absent from the chapels, large pictures of Jesus – the Master – hung in the main rooms of the Holy Order House and Novice Quarters. She was sure – or nearly sure – it was Jesus who had brought her to HOME.

Help me to understand, Lord, she prayed, and took the next step forward, no longer off the cliff, but now in mid-air.

CHAPTER SEVEN

Star Trek and a Jasmine-scented Milkmaid

Novice Stephen – July 1975

Stephen had been wondering lately how he'd wound up in this Holy Order of Mystical Evangelists. He wasn't holy, he wasn't particularly mystical (though he'd been called sensitive), and he was no evangelist nor would he be. He'd been an altar boy back home in Ireland until his teens, when the whole Catholic thing changed and stopped making sense. He still believed in God, though, in Jesus. He'd come to San Francisco from Donegal last year to play music and make a life for himself, but found out soon enough that it wasn't easy to do both at the same time. One of the Brothers found him high on cocaine at a club in the Fillmore, talked with him through the night, and bought him breakfast. A couple of classes and a strange kind of baptism later, he was in this three-month training on his way to who knew what. Maybe something better, maybe not.

The big issue right now was living with these women but not living with them, to put it as politely as possible. The priest folks all said this wasn't a monastery (thank you, Jesus) but sure it seemed like one. It was okay during the day when he was working – carpentry, mostly – he was good at that and it kept his mind off things. But then they all went home and showered, and the girls showered, and came downstairs all fresh and pink with their clean blouses and their wet hair pulled up in knots at their necks and little damp tendrils curling around their faces – and he could scarcely bear it and all. All the novices would sit together in the little front room for recreation – twenty of them in that little room all together for an hour. Sometimes they'd watch *Star Trek* since it was supposed to be about the coming of the New Age which was what everybody in HOME was all excited about. Sometimes they'd just talk.

There was this one named Althea, an Irish American girl with white skin and dark hair and green eyes, looking like his sisters but with American ways and with a difference in the way he looked at her and she looked at him. There were prettier girls here, sure, foxier as the Americans say, but this one had a brave and desperate look about her, like she'd run away with you in a heartbeat to find – whatever it was that you needed to find – because she needed it too.

She'd smile, kind of shy but he knew she wasn't shy when you got to know her. She could have shed a few pounds for his taste, but she was all right as she was, looking like a milkmaid from the old tales. One day she read a poem by Yeats, about wild swans at Cool, and it was music. Stephen had been to Cool and he'd seen the swans and suddenly he was so homesick and felt so close to this girl who was American but as Irish as could be and who smelled like jasmine and clean laundry and who looked almost as lonely as he felt – that he almost leaned over and kissed her right there in the front room of the novice quarters. Which would have been a bad scene, the worst. It didn't happen that day but it could, and then he could say goodbye to this gig.

What was he doing here anyhow? Sure it was good to get clean from the drugs and eat regular meals and have somebody looking out for him. But he was clean now and determined to stay that way, and he was never going to be one of these Brothers.

CHAPTER EIGHT

SATURDAYS

Althea – Summer 1975

Gradually Althea fell into the weekly pattern of novice life. Sunday was for worship and rest – no surprise there – and week days were for work and study with prayer at the start and finish, but Saturday had a new focus as the Day of Activity. The activities varied but they were all mandatory including, to Althea's distress, a morning of baseball in the park next door.

Althea had been severely asthmatic throughout her childhood, and the doctor had cautioned against strenuous exercise, so she had never participated in group sports but always waited on the sidelines. Besides that, she had been a high strung and moody child who preferred reading or deep conversation to playing any active games. As she grew older, she liked to walk and swim, but both of these were meditative, not competitive. That Saturday, she'd dressed in jeans and a tee shirt from the common closet, found a pair of sneakers that fit pretty well, and, groaning, trudged to the park, only to be "benched" under a tree for morning – bored, but grateful.

On Saturdays the novices each received an allowance – one dollar to spend in any way they chose. It seemed ludicrous to see these grown women and men, some of whom had had successful careers, excited about walking all by themselves to the corner store to buy an It's It – the famous San Francisco ice cream sandwich. Althea went along once. The ice cream sandwich tasted good but gave her sugar overload and a sick stomach. It was walking unsupervised on the sunny street, thinking her own thoughts, that was the real treat.

On Saturdays she could be alone, and most often she took advantage of the opportunity. Besides Sister Lois who was life-vowed and usually inaccessible, she made no friends, though she and the other female novices treated each other kindly. She wished she could get to know the male novice called Stephen, who was a musician from Ireland. He was cute and interesting, but he was also kind of brooding and kept to himself most of the time. Once he told her about the céilíthe back in Ireland, the music and dance parties he missed, and another time about playing music in the Fillmore district, how he wanted to make a living as a musician. Althea wondered if he might leave soon.

Sometimes by Saturday evening, she found herself wondering whether HOME was in fact a mistake. But then, she would ask herself, what was the alternative – going back to a life of confusion? So she stayed another week, and another.

CHAPTER NINE

A TEMPORARY COMMITMENT

Althea – August 1975

It was the last week in August, the final week of the novitiate. On Monday, Althea was presented with a collar which she would wear as Sister Althea, and she spent her recreation time that week embroidering the hidden base of the collar with her own symbol, a silver crescent moon, which to her meant the small reflection of God's light that she hoped to be in the world. On Saturday she would take student vows and be assigned to a site in one of several states where she would spend her student year. This was also a week for departures of another kind.

On Wednesday morning when she returned to her dorm room after breakfast, one of her roommates, the petite brunette from Texas who had always been called Perpetua, was packing her suitcase while belting out "Stand by Your Man."

"Perpetua – what's going on?"

She stopped, turned to look Althea in the eye, grinned, and said in a broad drawl, "Freedom, my friend, freedom. I am going home. I am going to hug my mother and kiss that man I left last spring, kiss him like he has never been kissed before. Oh, and my name is Tammy. Not Perpetua. And most definitely not Sister anything. I am now and forever little Tammy from Waxahachie, and so, so happy to be. What's your real name, anyhow, and where's your home?"

"Tricia, Tricia Riley," she answered, surprising herself at how easily the answer came and how she did not argue with the phrases, *your real name, your home.* "Not sure where I'd say I'm from, Per – uh, Tammy."

Tammy grinned. "Right. This is supposed to be your home, isn't it? We're supposed to let go of where we're from, and we're supposed to trust them all to take us where we need to go, right? Well, just be sure you know where you *want* to be going, Tricia Riley, and take a hard look at where they're trying to take you."

Tammy gave Althea a hug and breezed out the door.

The next day, sure enough, Stephen, the novice from Ireland, was at the door with his suitcase.

"Cheers, luv."

"You too? Why, Stephen? Don't you want to serve anymore?"

"Eh, not so sure I ever wanted to serve, luv. I needed to straighten up a bit, and I did. God knows my name and all – it's Aiden, by the way – and I don't need all of this. It's high time I made some music again, but without messing around getting high like before. I'll miss seeing you though. Give us a hug before we go?"

She did give Stephen – Aiden – a hug, hoping no one saw, and he held her a moment longer than was friendly until she gently disengaged.

"Go with God, Aiden. Make some beautiful music."

"Sure I will. Be happy, luv."

Before the end of the week, four more novices had left. It was a small group who stood before the altar that Friday evening to take their temporary vows of poverty, purity, humility, obedience, and service. In her sermon, Reverend Ursula told them that they were the chosen few, that the others had not responded to the High Calling, but that they had the faith and courage to respond.

Chosen...faith and courage. Althea's heart leapt as she thought of herself in this way – not lost, not confused, not failing, but chosen. Watching the others go, and especially witnessing a new confidence and sense of direction in Perpetua/Tammy and Stephen/Aiden, had shaken her. But where would she go? What or who would be waiting for her return? No faithful man like Tammy's. No blooming career like Aiden's. And what if those who left were making a terrible mistake in rejecting their calling? No, whatever new misgivings Althea may have entertained, she stood with the "chosen few" and took the vows. She would strive to be worthy of the High Calling.

PART THREE

STUDENT TRAINING

CHAPTER ONE

A HOME?

Sister Althea – Fall 1975, Denver, Colorado

Scanning the waiting room of the Greyhound bus station in Denver, Althea spotted a tall, sturdily built red-headed Scot of a man. He looked to be about forty, and was smoking a pipe while perusing a newspaper. He was wearing a black clerical shirt and pants under a tweed jacket. She approached him shyly.

"Good evening. I'm Sister Althea."

He glanced up from his paper. "Yes, of course, and I am Father Edwin, your House Father. Do you have any luggage to retrieve? The bus is late and we need to get back to the center for dinner."

He surely doesn't waste words, Sister Althea thought. "One checked suitcase," she answered with what she hoped was the brevity he was looking for.

Conversation on the drive to the Student Center was sparse, but she tried to relate as well as she could to this man who would be holding her fate in his hands for the next year.

"Have you been in Denver long, Father Edwin?"

"For a year."

"Do you like it here?"

"I am fulfilling the service I have been assigned. It's a two year assignment. My fiancé is at another center."

"Ah." What else could she say? He was clearly serving out his time. She tried a different subject. "Where are you from?"

"Tennessee. Clarksville, outside of Nashville."

"I've heard of it. There's a song, right? 'Last Train to Clarksville?'"

Father Edwin raised a bushy red eyebrow. "Different Clarksville."

And then silence. Great, she thought, another silent, absent father. Hopefully this one wasn't mean.

After what seemed a very long time, they parked in front of a large and stately stone house which she would later learn was a Silver Rush mansion. They ascended the wide staircase and entered a warm wood-panelled front hall which smelled deliciously of roasting chicken.

"Sister Sandra!" Father Edwin called loudly. A short and full-figured woman in an apron walked swiftly to meet them. Interestingly, she was also a freckled red-head and might have been taken for Father Edwin's biological sister. Approaching Sister Althea and smiling, she reached out her hand.

"Sister Sandra, the Cook," she said breathlessly, brushing back the tendrils from her damp face. "And you must be Sister Althea. Welcome to Denver. Let's get you settled – only ten minutes until dinnertime, which is never late."

"It smells delicious," Althea said, smiling.

"Good. Roast chicken tonight in honor of the arrival of our new students. I hope you're hungry."

She grabbed the large blue suitcase, nearly as big as she was, and whisked Sister Althea up a wooden staircase. Another large hallway formed the second floor landing.

"This is the floor where the female students sleep and where I have a room." She nodded to a closed door near the top of the stairs. "Father Edwin and Brother Matthew, who is our life-vowed Steward, have rooms on the third floor where the male students sleep. That is also where the chapel is." She led the way to a spacious, high-ceilinged bedroom furnished with three sets of bunk beds. "You're the last student arriving for this room, so the bottom bunk right here is yours. There are two bathrooms on this floor and a third on the main floor if the others are occupied, which they often are with more than twenty students here. Try to use the one closest to your room when possible. Otherwise, women students may use the one close to my room on the other side of the landing when it is not occupied, as long as you leave it clean and tidy. It's a good idea to get up early if you want to shower. Right now this one closest to your room should be free. You've got about five minutes to freshen up if you like. Your towel and wash cloth are there on the bunk. The dining room's the second door on the left downstairs – follow the aroma." Winking, she set down the suitcase and breezed out the door.

Sister Althea washed quickly and went downstairs, thinking she liked this high-energy life-vowed sister.

The dining room, like the other rooms she glimpsed on the first floor, was appointed in light oak with a high ceiling, hardwood floor, and many tall windows. Student-vowed Brothers and Sisters stood behind their chairs around the long dining table, with Father Edwin at the head, Sister Sandra at his left, and at his right a tall, smiling brother with a life-vowed collar and cross.

"Ah, Sister Althea – please take the empty place. Brother Matthew, students, this is Sister Althea who has come from San Francisco," Father Edwin said, with what passed for a smile.

"Hello everyone," she said.

A buzz of greetings and smiles followed until Father Edwin raised his hand to signal silence.

All assembled bowed their heads while Father Edwin, Brother Matthew, and Sister Sandra intoned the Prayer of HOME:

"I strive to be a Nameless Wanderer, …

Why nameless, Althea wondered. Didn't Mary Magdalene recognize Jesus Christ in the garden after His Resurrection because He called her by her name? Isn't a name important? That's part of what Tammy and Aiden were trying to tell her before they left the novice center – their names were important to them; *her* name was important to them. What's your real name, Tammy had asked, and she'd answered, "Tricia. My name is Tricia."

"…Like the fool of the Tarot,
perfect and self-sufficient…

But how could a fool be perfect or self-sufficient? Were people supposed to be completely self-sufficient? What about relying on God?

"Only the Self-realized can understand…"

Maybe that was it – she was too unenlightened to understand.

The prayer continued for several verses, mostly paraphrasing parts of the Gospels, and Althea's thoughts drifted, but the last verse recaptured her attention:

"Let me be received into this holy family, to be the servant of all, to hear Thy great call…"

Received into this family. A servant. The great call. Yes – by whatever name she was called, she was in a place where she would belong.

The prayer was over, dinner began, and she hadn't eaten since breakfast in San Francisco. The roast chicken was homemade delicious, and the other students kept up a steady flow of questions so that she scarcely had a thought to herself before collapsing into bed that night.

She lay on her back in the silent darkness she shared with five women whose names she didn't yet remember, all of whom were also strangers in this place and who, for all she knew, might also be balancing doubt and hope, fear and what she wanted to believe was inspiration. The slats of the top bunk above her felt too close, pressing in on her. She closed her eyes to see the sparks of light she had always seen since she was a little girl – sometimes dancing, sometimes pulsing. She had learned in her novitiate to call these "yods" (the tenth and smallest letter of the Hebrew alphabet and a term for the finger of God). Maybe God's finger was upon her tonight. But then, maybe it had always been…?

CHAPTER TWO

SERVICE AND A WRITING JOB

Sister Althea – September 1975, Denver, Colorado

One of the first tasks the students were given was to find a job so that they could contribute to the economy of the house. Each morning after breakfast, Sister Althea would scan the newspaper, hoping to find something that would match with her skills, but it wasn't easy. She was highly literate, but hadn't finished a degree or gotten any sort of formal training, and the want ads had no openings for poets.

The pressure mounted daily and by the second week Father Edwin was asking each morning at breakfast whether she had any interviews set up, or at least some leads. Finally, on Thursday afternoon of the second week, she was excited to find an opening for a copy editor at a small local newspaper called *Platte Press*.

"Father Edwin, I've found a good job," she called out, hurrying into his office. "It's at a newspaper."

"Let me see," Father Edwin said, taking the classifieds from her hand. He read the circled announcement and frowned. "This is only part time."

"That's true, but it pays pretty well. It would be a great opportunity for me to write, which is something I'm good at. It could help me develop a career."

Red-haired, heavy-set Father Edwin seldom smiled, and he wasn't smiling now.

"That is not the goal, Sister Althea. You have taken a vow of service, and the goal is to serve your brothers and sisters, not to fulfill your personal ambitions."

Her heart sank and she looked at her feet.

"A student having a part time job would be highly unusual," he continued.

"I could spend the rest of the day helping out here. I helped in the kitchen when I was a novice."

Father Edwin pursed his full lips and looked again at the job listing. "It's true that this pays well above minimum wage. What did you do in the kitchen in San Francisco?"

"I helped the cook with prep work, setting up, and serving food. I worked in restaurants before I met the Holy Order, too, in the kitchen and serving."

"And you haven't found any restaurant work advertised?

"No, not during the day when I'm supposed to be working. Only ads for experienced cooks, which is not really what I am."

"Hmmm."

Sister Althea breathed in and out deeply. A potential paid writing job – dream come true – was in the hands of this man who apparently gave little or no thought to what she wanted, and frankly was kind of scary. If she had typecast someone in the role of her father, she couldn't have done better than Father Edwin.

After what seemed like many moments, he finally said, "Very well. Set up an interview. I will inform the cook, Sister Hannah. You can report to her at six a.m. tomorrow to help set up breakfast before morning prayers. You will need to rise at 5:30. Don't be late."

"Thank you, thank you, Father Edwin! This is going to be great."

Father Edwin nodded curtly and turned to the papers on his desk.

Sister Althea called *The Platte Press* right away and set up an interview for 9:00 am the next morning, the earliest she would be able to get there by bus after prayers and breakfast. She had wanted for a long time to work for a newspaper, and had even planned to study journalism before her father refused to give her any support. She would be paid to write!

Her enthusiasm lasted until she arrived at *The Platte Press* the following morning.

The office was in a small storefront near the Platte River that gave the paper its name. Sam, the editor, was a tired-looking man of maybe sixty or so, though it was hard to tell from the face behind his full, greying beard. He spoke through his teeth which clenched a smoking pipe.

"Okay, miss, why should I hire you?"

"I can write."

"Oh yeah? What have you written?"

"Poetry, mostly, but some articles and stories. A play a couple of years ago."

"Nah, none of that counts for much on a newspaper. Have you ever written ad copy?"

"Ad copy? No – I thought I'd be writing articles. I've done some of that for my high school paper."

"Nope. I write the articles. I need somebody to get paid advertising for the paper. That means calling businesses, selling them on placing ads, and then writing the ad copy. Do you think you can do that?"

"I guess so," Sister Althea said, realizing too late how unenthusiastic she sounded. She hoped Sam hadn't noticed the disappointment in her voice.

"How much school do you have?"

"Three years of college. Dean's List. Editor of the literary magazine."

"Can you write clean prose?"

This was humiliating – she was published poet! – clean prose indeed! She didn't dignify the question with a verbal answer, but raised an eyebrow and nodded.

Sam must have been desperate for help because he hired her during the interview and asked her to start that morning.

"You can sit over there." He nodded to a small wooden desk littered with old newspapers, merchants' flyers, and legal pads filled with scrawled notes.

Sister Althea could not stand a mess, and immediately began tidying the papers into a large metal wastebasket.

"I wouldn't do that if I were you," Sam hissed through the teeth that clenched his pipe.

"No?"

"Those are your leads, young lady."

"Ah. So...I need to call the businesses listed in these flyers and...?"

"And the businesses listed in the back copies of our paper there. You can cross-reference with the notes on those pads left by your predecessor."

"Oh, who had this job before me?"

"Don't remember his name. He only lasted a week."

Sister Althea had nothing to say to this. It was 10:30 a.m., two and a half hours left on her four hour shift. Grabbing the flyers and the notes, she soon deduced that her predecessor hadn't had much luck with his cold calling. No matter, she would start fresh. She ripped the notes from a legal pad, sharpened a couple of pencils, seized the handle of the black desk phone and started dialing.

CHAPTER THREE

She Doesn't Seem to Fit

Father Edwin – September 1975, Denver, Colorado

Sister Althea was becoming a concern for Father Edwin. Everything about her was an exception, an adjustment, a reason for reprimand – in short, a pain. He had twelve young women and ten young men to shepherd, and he did not have time for all that. She wasn't disobedient exactly. In fact, she showed up for chapel and class and duties on time, she worked hard, she spoke respectfully. She just couldn't seem to understand the unspoken rules, the expectations. She would sit in the library during study time with the correct book on her lap and her eyes on the page, but he had noticed that it might be the same page for half an hour. When he questioned her, she apologized and said it was difficult for her to concentrate. Did she have problems reading, or problems with her eyes, he'd asked. No, not at all, she'd said. The problem was with her mind. It was so difficult to focus; she would drift off into her imagination and it was sometimes a long while before she would realize it. She didn't know how to control it. What could he do about that, when she seemed as concerned as he was? He'd seen similar issues with students recruited from the streets who'd been traumatized or who had done drugs for years, but her files didn't show anything like that. In fact, she seemed fairly fresh-faced and healthy.

Then there was the way she would dress and fix her hair. Obviously all the sisters were meant to present themselves simply, but he had to remind Sister Althea of this repeatedly. Even at home in her student garb, although she would pull back her hair into the standard French twist and secure it with a large barrette as the others did, tendrils of hair would always come loose and curl around her face, and he would have to send her to fix them. When she dressed in street clothes for her job it was worse. How she could put together stylish outfits from the boxes of shared hand-me-downs was beyond him. They weren't supposed to do that. Once last week, he'd lost his temper with her over a fitted black suit with a red scarf which she said she thought looked professional. From her response, it didn't seem as if she were purposely trying to look alluring, but the effect was the same as if she were. He'd raised his voice and told her to go and change immediately. Of course, he shouldn't have done that; she was probably just a naïve kid, but then he was only human and trying to draw the appropriate boundaries, not only for the male brothers, but frankly for himself.

Headquarters had placed him here in this house to be responsible for a dozen young women, not to mention eight young men who were bound to notice the young women, and they had separated him from Sister Barbara for two years – another whole year before the mission was completed! Why hadn't they allowed him to marry Barbara and bring her with him? When he'd asked, they simply reminded him of his and Barbara's vows and said they were needed where they were assigned.

Ten more months to go.

CHAPTER FOUR

Comparative Religions, Revisited

Sister Althea – Denver, October 1975

Several years before, when she'd first started college, Sister Althea had studied comparative religions in a formal class, reading classic texts such as Huston Smith's *Religions of the World*, but this had been a conceptual, academic approach. Later, after leaving the Catholic Church, she had begun to search for truth in anthropology and religions, and this had been a more personal quest. Now, though, she was taught that all religions should be united in a new age of enlightenment, that no scripture contained ultimate truth (and how could that be so?), that many avatars had come to earth, and that the only ultimate truth was to be found in the laws of nature which transcend human interpretation (but wasn't nature fallen along with human beings?)

The Truth is to be found within each person, her teachers said; no one needs to be taught dogmas but rather needs to learn to remember; each person has lived many lives and must reach to remember his or her ultimate being. When she had first encountered HOME, most of the teachings had sounded basically Christian, but with a twist toward the New Age, and a foundation in recent revelation. Now what she was being taught was wildly radical.

It was true that she had found glimmers of truth in many faiths. She deeply respected the attempt of ancient Egyptians to worship one God called Aten – the sun – and the reverence of Native Americans for Wakan Tanka, the Great Spirit. So many people had reached toward truth, perhaps had even received revelation of truth. At the same time, she knew that the various religions had widely differing beliefs. Now, as she was seeing their differences in detail, she wondered – how could they possibly be brought into one faith without compromising – or even abandoning -- what each sincerely believed? Yes, that was the path of convinced conversion, but of compromise? Althea (as Tricia) had learned in her study of literature that a good translation is key – that translations could differ so widely as to change meaning entirely. Father Peter was translating from the Master – God! – and then others were translating from him. Did the Master really reveal a plan of uniting all faiths, or had someone misunderstood or miscommunicated along the way? She struggled through the required reading, and held to the hope that if the Master did have a plan of uniting all faiths, it would gradually become clear to her. Fortunately, no tests or essays were required in this student year, and she was left the freedom of her own thoughts on the subject of uniting all faiths. If Father Edwin couldn't see her mind, he couldn't censure her.

What did require oral reading and discussion were the books written by Father Peter containing "direct revelation from the Master." Each Saturday morning after breakfast, the student Brothers and Sisters would gather in the library to study and explore these teachings together. As she listened and tried to understand, Sister Althea often absorbed these ideas without discerning truth from falsehood, like a starving person devouring a meal laced with ground glass. Direct revelation from the Master Who had chosen her and given her a life!

Some of the phrasing of these books of revelation was scriptural-sounding and stirred her heart:

"There is mundane service on the earth, giving to man the things he needs. There is also spiritual service on the earth, and this is the Work."

"The life of the Master Jesus is a type for those who would follow Him."

"Embrace the High Calling."

In discussing the teachings more clearly connected with Christianity, especially about taking care of the poor and speaking the truth, she often joined enthusiastically in the discussion. On the other hand, reincarnation as a given – the Master Teachers as reincarnated apostles and they themselves as having had many previous lives – was not a concept that was clear to her. The science of mind as a spiritual practice was so unfamiliar that she kept silent and wondered if she would ever understand.

Then there were the teachings that jarred her, and that she questioned openly.

"'Those who are called engage in a transformational process referred to as alchemy,'" Fr. Edwin read.

"Is alchemy Christian?" Sister Althea asked.

"If the Master directs it, how can it be anything else?"

"Does the Master direct it? We haven't heard His words about that."

"We can be certain that Fr. Paul did."

There were many questions like this, questions without actual answers, which she would turn over in thought with varying levels of distress when she had a moment to herself, usually while staring at the mattress close above her head, just before falling asleep.

A directive that haunted her was: "Mastering visualization is important to your spiritual attainment." This had become a serious issue, since after the better part of a year she had still had no visions whatsoever.

Sister Althea and the other students were also taught the first twenty-one cards of the Tarot deck as a set of spiritual milestones on the Path of Initiation that a person must follow in his or her return to the Creator. They painted Tarot card templates with tempura paints as a meditation, and Althea discovered that she liked The Empress card the best. She painted the Empress's gown in rich green and gold and wondered whether she herself had been royalty in a past life. It was certainly a flattering thought. She had some vague recollection from Catholic school that Tarot and fortune-telling were forbidden superstitions, but maybe that was just a Catholic thing. If the Master told Father Peter to teach Tarot, it must be important in some way the Catholics didn't understand.

Every weekday morning at 7:00 a.m., after an hour's work as kitchen assistant, Sister Althea would join the others in chapel to meditate, and then to attend a "Mass," followed by a simple breakfast, house chores, and her outside job. Though sometimes it was difficult to rise so early, she welcomed the discipline and regularity, and the belief that her life had purpose. She would take the bus home after working at the newspaper, and arrive about two o'clock. That gave her about an hour for exercise or reading and cleaning the second floor bathrooms before she reported to the kitchen to help prepare dinner.

By that late afternoon hour, she was often quite tired, but Sister Sandra's company cheered her. The little life-vowed cook was so energetic and kind. Her clear directions were easy to follow, and Sister Althea liked to work beside her to clean, chop, slice, sauté, mix, bake, and broil. Food itself as God gave it was so beautiful and simple, a good break from selling advertising.

CHAPTER FIVE

SATURDAYS WITH SISTER ALTHEA

Sister Karen – October, 1975

For Sister Karen, Saturday afternoons were a time to be normal in the very abnormal place that the Denver Student Center was for her. She'd completed her bachelor's degree in sign language the previous year, but she wasn't ready to settle down in a job yet. She'd grown up as a church-going Episcopalian in Corpus Christi, her beloved home town in south Texas perched on the shore of the Gulf of Mexico, and she had never felt the need to escape it. Similarly, she hadn't stopped believing as she'd always believed, but she wanted more self-knowledge than she was getting by going to church once a week, so when she met one of the Brothers the previous spring, she'd decided to give HOME a try, to achieve some spiritual growth.

The degree of discipline and control during her novitiate in Atlanta had come as a shock, but some of the life-vowed sisters had told her that more freedom would come gradually in time, and she was willing to give it a try at least for a while. All the same, there was a beautiful world out there, she was determined to experience it, and she preferred to do that with a companion. After interviewing a number of the other student sisters, she decided on Sister Althea.

Sister Althea had made some interesting comments during classes. She could think for herself, and she wasn't shy about asking questions. She didn't have that glazed look in her eyes that some of the others had, though at first Sister Karen wasn't sure about her because she seemed to be struggling with some kind of sorrow or mental pain. After taking a risk talking with her a couple of times, she discovered that the cryptic Althea was sometimes able to emerge from that painful place inside herself, and that made Sister Karen happy.

Saturday afternoons were their times to explore. After the prayers and the breakfast and the interminable class about who they were supposed to become, Karen and Althea grabbed bicycles and remembered what they were at that moment – twenty-something-year-old women in a new and interesting place.

They started their Saturday adventures by walking through the park near the Student Center. It was a pretty place, with statues and an amphitheater where Althea took the stage and recited a poem by Byron about the west wind, and after that Karen was sure they'd be friends.

They branched out gradually in their explorations, riding along the Platte and stopping for coffee at a cozy café that overlooked the river. Or they'd save up their two-dollar weekly allowance (how exciting to have double the allowance now that they were students) for a couple of weeks and have Denver omelets in the oak-paneled dining room of the Hilton hotel downtown. A couple of times they got really ambitious and bicycled all the way to Boulder, nearly thirty miles, to walk around the college and have wine and cheese at a cool little restaurant before hoisting their bicycles onto a bus headed back to Denver.

Sister Karen wasn't at all sure she'd be staying with HOME for long, but Saturdays reminded her that this was her decision and hers alone, not a thing to be assumed. She hoped sincerely that Althea knew that about her own decisions, too.

CHAPTER SIX

A Failure in the World

Sister Althea, November 1975

Within a week, Althea had overcome her reluctance to call strangers to attempt to sell them advertising for *The Platte Review* and she was making up to twenty calls a day. Every once in a while, the sale was successful and she had the chance to do what she considered her real job, which was to write the ad copy.

Sam, the editor, sat behind his desk watching her while he did whatever it was editors did. In Sam's case this was apparently to smoke his pipe and scrutinize Althea. After all, he was paying her $3.50 an hour, almost twice the minimum wage, as he frequently reminded her. But Althea didn't need to be motivated from the outside; actually being paid to write, even to write ad copy, was enough to make her throw herself into her work.

The problem was that *The Platte Press* was no *Denver Post* nor would it ever be. It was a weekly with a circulation of under 3,000 at best, and the number of local businesses willing to pay for advertising in its pages was limited, no matter what Sam, in his myopic dedication and faith, believed.

The Wednesday before Thanksgiving, just before her shift was ending, the inevitable happened.

"Young lady, we need to have a talk."

Althea's heart sank.

"You're a hard worker; there's no denying that, but you're just not achieving the results we need here."

"Really? I sold five ads this week."

"And that's not enough. Ten ads running for a month or more would just about allow the paper to stay in the black. I'm sorry, young lady, but I've had to find somebody more experienced."

Tears came to Althea's eyes but she breathed deeply to push them back. He'd already replaced her.

"When will my last day be?"

"I can write you your last check today."

Today. What would she tell Father Edwin who'd been so reluctant to let her take this job in the first place? Leaving the newspaper office in a daze, she stopped at a café to search the want ads in *The Denver Post*. There wasn't much there so close to the Christmas holidays, but she did an announcement for a temporary holiday job at a florist. That would at least be something to keep Father Edwin's ire at bay. She called from a payphone.

"No, I don't actually have florist experience but I love flowers and I've made arrangements for church."

Silence.

"And I've always been told I'm a hard worker."

"Okay. If you don't mind lifting bucket of water and stripping stems, you can come by now so I can meet you."

Now? It was nearly two o'clock, the bus ride back to the student center took more than half an hour even if the bus were on time, and she was due in the kitchen at three to begin dinner preparation. Could she call the Student Center? No, because Father Edwin would surely be the one to answer. Better to apologize, job in hand, than to ask permission, she decided.

Twenty minutes later she was opening the door of a local florist shop, which thankfully was located on the way back to the Student Center. The owner's name was Pam, a plump blonde woman who smiled in greeting.

"Tricia?"

"Yes, hello." The students used their given names at their places of employment to make legal matters clear, though Sam had never called her anything but "Miss" or "young lady."

"So you love flowers?"

"I do. My grandfather had a beautiful garden and so did my mother. I've always liked to help tend the flowers and make bouquets, and I did arrangements for the church when I lived at home."

"Where's home?"

"I grew up in New York, in a small town outside of Buffalo, but I guess right now Denver is my home."

"Are you going to school here?"

"Yes, at a nondenominational seminary." This was the response the students had been told to give.

"Hmm. I didn't know of a seminary in town."

"It's a small one. I'm here for a year."

"I'll probably need you for only about four or five weeks, until Christmas. Will that work for you?"

"Yes, it's perfect. I can look for a long-term job in the meantime."

"Can you start tomorrow? Eight to noon, Monday through Friday?"

And that was that; she gave Sam as a local reference because even though he'd fired her he knew she could work hard.

When Althea arrived at the Student Center a little after four o'clock, Father Edwin met her at the door, hands on hips, his face as red as his hair.

Before he could speak, Althea blurted, "I got a job," and launched into her story. As she spoke, Father Edwin's scowl of anger changed to a scowl of concentration, and finally to a frustrated wince.

"Why didn't you call? Do you know that I'm responsible for your welfare? Sister Sandra and I were worried sick. In another hour we would have called the police."

"I know, but I couldn't tell you I'd lost my job before I had another one. You didn't want me to take the job at the newspaper in the first place and I thought you'd be so disappointed in me." She looked at her shoes. When she looked up again, she saw something new on Father Edwin's face – compassion, maybe even forgiveness.

Pam proved to be a cheerful if demanding boss. Althea's duties that first morning and three times a week afterward began with helping Pam to unload the truck when she arrived from the floral market, filling about a hundred buckets with water and carrying them to the workroom or the cooler. On a large stainless steel table, she cut an inch from the stems of the flowers using a very sharp knife, and stripped off the lower leaves. Pam explained that the lower leaves would rot in the water buckets, so stripping the stems kept the flowers fresher.

Pam created arrangements every day, and for this Althea became a messenger. Pam stood before an array of vases and florist foam while calling out directions to Althea.

"I need a bucket of white hydrangeas, one of red long-stemmed roses, one of baby's breath, and one of boxwood."

Sometimes the choices were more exotic.

"What does arthurium look like?"

"That's anthurium. Like a red lily pad with a yellow tongue."

"What a beautiful image. You could write some decent poetry if you wanted to, Pam."

"Ha! In my spare time, right?"

No, not in spare time, Althea thought, but in stolen time, which was how she wrote poetry now. Still, the flowers were poetry of a sort, and she loved to watch as Pam's skilled fingers grouped them into colors, sizes, and textures that complemented one another perfectly.

CHAPTER SEVEN

Christmas at HOME

Sister Althea, December 1975

All over downtown, Christmas lights were sparkling, carols were broadcast into the streets, and Althea had to admit that she was homesick. It didn't make sense at all. She had left her messed up home more than three years ago, knowing that she couldn't build any kind of life there that she wanted to live. Yet she missed her mother, and Rita, and Timmy, and Bridget. She missed Jana too, though Jana hadn't replied to any of the letters she had sent since the writing ban of her novitiate ended.

She was pretty sure she remembered images of past Christmases in the rosy light of what she'd always wished for them to be, but that wasn't helping her heart. "I'll be HOME for Christmas, you can count on me," Sister Sandra sang as she prepared dinner. Frankly, it was annoying the way Sister Sandra assumed that Althea – and everyone at the Student Center – was home. Sister Sandra was kind, but she was definitely a company woman who walked and talked the line. In four months, Althea had hardly gotten to know anyone but Sister Karen. Karen was a real friend but a friend did not make a home. Nor did a House Father who was nearly as intimidating and controlling as her own father had been when she was younger. Her mother and her sisters and her brother were home at Christmastime, but how would she be able even to send gifts to her family when she had so little money saved?

The answer came one afternoon as she was taking the garbage to the dumpster behind the florist shop. There, on top of the dumpster garbage, was a twenty-dollar bill – a fortune! She looked around but saw no one. Picking it up, she went to find Pam.

"On top of the garbage? How strange."

"Is it yours?"

"Nope. I think it's yours, Tricia."

Oh, the shopping spree she had at the five and ten store. Little wooden ornaments, mini manicure sets, travel sizes of cosmetics, a paperback book – something for each member of her family, and something for her friend Sister Karen and each of her roommates. There was enough left to buy a roll of gold wrapping paper and sparkly white ribbon. She put her family's gifts in a small box and mailed it the next day, in plenty of time to arrive for Christmas. On Christmas Eve, she placed a small treasure on each of her roommates' pillows and on Sister Karen's pillow.

On Christmas day, after the service and a special breakfast, all the students gathered in the living room around the tall, lighted tree to sing Christmas carols. Sister Sandra and Father Edwin distributed a gift to each of them. Althea's was a blue leather wallet which she liked a lot. She looked around at all the smiling faces singing about peace on earth and goodwill toward men. It was Christmas, sort of.

CHAPTER EIGHT

OBEDIENCE

Father Edwin, January 1976

Father Edwin was not looking forward to the conversation he had to have with Sister Althea. He could see that she was trying very hard within the confines of her understanding, but there was so much she did not understand. This was a spiritual order of the highest caliber, but she seemed to treat it as a kind of church group where, yes, she worked hard and prayed, but she didn't see that the life she was leading this year was a means to Self-Realization. At base, this was what HOME was about, not the prayers or the service work, though of course the Chosen had a duty to serve the less fortunate. HOME was about the path to enlightenment. She just did not seem to get that.

Take that newspaper job, for instance. It was all about her desire to be a writer, but she had to put those ambitions behind her for a time. Later, of course, once she was Enlightened, she could choose from many different professions. Sister Clare was in medical school, but Self-Realization and life vows came first, and Sister Clare had never argued with that. All of them had to put in the work – the Spiritual Work, as the Master had revealed to Father Peter:

"There is mundane service on the earth, giving to man the things he needs. There is also spiritual service on the earth, and this is the Work."

The Master also revealed that visualization is key to the Spiritual Work, but had this student been working with visualization? No. When questioned about what she did in the Chapel, she said, again and again through the Novitiate and the last five months as a student, that she prayed, that she asked that any images be only from God. She did not understand that she needed to go within actively and seize Illumination – and then the Light would come.

That was the long-term issue. The short-term issue was that she needed to find a job immediately. Not a cushy job or an impressive job, which could take quite a while to find for someone who dropped out of college before finishing her Bachelor's degree, but a regular full time job, five days a week. For pity's sake, he himself had an engineering degree and during his student year he had worked on a construction crew because it was good, steady temporary work.

Sister Althea would resist his choosing for her, of course, and want to choose for herself, but he could not be concerned with that. The students had taken five vows, some of which, like humility, were difficult to achieve, but obedience was quite straightforward, and Sister Althea needed to obey his directive. If the students did not obey, how could he be responsible for them?

He opened the Sunday paper to the want ads and began searching. When Sister Althea arrived half an hour later for their appointment, he had found a job that would work well.

"Sister Althea, now that the New Year has arrived, you need a new job, and I've found one for you."

Sister Althea looked down, took a visibly deep breath, and looked up at Father Edwin. She wasn't arguing – yet.

"There's an opening for a nurse's aide at the Parkside Convalescent Home very close to here. The hours are eight to four-thirty with a half hour lunch. I would like for you to apply today."

"But Father Edwin, I don't have any medical experience."

"That's not a problem. What is required is strength, hard work, and compassion. The job posting says that you will be giving patients showers, changing their beds and their clothes, feeding them, and taking care of other duties as assigned." Clear, straight-forward – no room for argument. And no pushback yet, only a doubt. Now to appeal to her self-respect – can she do it?

"Do you think you can handle that, Sister Althea?"

After an uncomfortable silence during which she looked at the floor, she met his eyes and answered, "I'll apply this afternoon."

CHAPTER NINE

SERVICE

Sister Althea, February 1976

The job at Parkside Convalescent Home was actually better than she had feared. The director was a kind and intelligent woman who recognized what she called Sister Althea's "communication skills," and promised to find opportunities for her to offer emotional support to some of the patients. Meanwhile, there were the basic chores such as emptying bedpans, changing beds, giving patients showers – all the mundane work she had expected. She was surprised to find that, with notable exceptions such as an angry man with dementia who fought her throughout his shower, or a sick woman who soiled her bed several times a day, she liked the work. It was simple hard work which left little or no time to think of herself. It was clearly service, and hadn't she vowed to serve? Maybe the newspaper job wasn't actually service. Maybe God had worked through Father Edwin to give her this job.

After she had showered and dressed a patient, she sometimes had the time to sit by his or her bed and listen. Often what the patients had to say was a heartbreaking plea for their family members to visit them. Sometimes, on a good day, someone would talk about the distant past that was so vivid to them, much more vivid than what had happened last week. They would talk about their parents, jumping rope or playing jacks, sledding, first dances, their friends at school. As she listened, Sister Althea would pray for the person, for peace, for forgiveness, for heaven.

She had to work two Sundays a month, which she had thought would be terrible because of missing services, but Sundays at Parkside turned out to be her favorite work days, and that was mainly because of Angela, the RN. Angela was a tall, dark-haired woman in her forties, a mother of four with a generously sized body and a more generous heart. She told Sister Althea that she was a Christian and liked to go to church on Sundays, but didn't mind working twice a month because, after all, Jesus was everywhere.

Once they had cared for the elderly patients, Angela would gather the mentally challenged residents in a circle in the recreation room and pull out her guitar. These were mostly younger, permanent residents who were not sick but needed a safe place to live. Angela would sing, "What a Friend We Have in Jesus," "Go Tell It on the Mountain," "Michael Row Your Boat Ashore," and lots of other spirituals. Angela was brilliant. These residents knew all her songs and sang along with huge smiles on their faces. She definitely created a Sunday service in its own right.

Angela was as funny as she was kind. She could find the humor in their situation without making the joke at anyone's expense. Later in the day, she'd wheel the med cart through the halls chanting, "Drugs, get your drugs!" for Althea's amusement and her own. When a resident became particularly difficult, she would look at Sister Althea and smile a silly smile. She seemed to love all of them. She became a friend, and Sister Althea didn't have a lot of those.

CHAPTER TEN

A Healer?

Angela Riva, RN, March 1976

This aide they'd assigned her was a piece of work. She liked her, no question, but the girl was no nurse's aide. Kind to the patients? Yes. Hard worker? Yes. But no medical worker. Tricia Riley was a dreamer, a poet (sometimes she'd read her work to the residents, and it wasn't bad), and a wannabe saint (the kind of angel with a crooked halo and mischievous look that you sometimes see on Christmas cards.) She didn't have a practical bone in her body. The showers she gave the patients were interminable, and Angela had to explain that thorough did not mean exhaustive when it came to hygiene for a basically well person. Then it took Tricia fifteen minutes to dress a resident, even one who wasn't resistant. Feedings were a zoo, with more food on the mentally challenged residents' faces and clothing than inside them; sometimes Angela would need to ask for additional meals to make up for what was lost.

With all of this, Angela never complained to the director. Why? Because she would rather have one inefficient and caring Tricia than both of the night aides, who did the bare minimum in record time and ignored the residents to chat with each other and eat. Oh, she had dropped by to see how things were going around midnight, and found residents lying in their own feces, or weeping silently with bedsores when they hadn't been turned since that morning. Those aides she did report, and they were replaced with somewhat better workers. Somewhat. It was difficult to get excellent work from uneducated people making minimum wage, especially when the night nurse was also pretty disengaged, but the other nurses were beyond Angela's jurisdiction.

So Angela picked up a bit of the grunt work from Tricia – a shower here, a feeding there – while Tricia often spent her breaks wheeling residents out into the garden and listening to their stories of long ago. It was an okay tradeoff. Tricia would be with them only until August, when she would maybe go and fulfill some of her dreams. She said her other name in her religious order was Althea. Angela told her that was the official name for the Rose of Sharon tree, which was one of her favorite plants. Hers was white, and gave hundreds of blooms in the spring and summer. Cool, Tricia Althea said, she wanted to see it, and added that her name also meant "healer". Angela guessed that fit her. Not a medical healer, but in some sense a healer all the same.

CHAPTER ELEVEN

A FINALE

Sister Althea – March 1976

On a Saturday night in March, Sister Karen surprised Althea with an invitation to a planetarium show based on Isaac Asimov's story, "The Last Question." It was a stunning presentation. As they reclined under the huge dome, they witnessed angelic beings asking each other with great compassion for those on earth, "Can entropy be reversed? Can entropy be reversed?" Of all the issues Sister Althea worried about, the gradual dissipation of the known universe was a new one. It was a question answered in the story by an enormous network of computers that had absorbed all human knowledge. It declared, "Let there be light," and there was light. Of course, the premise was blasphemous but Sister Althea didn't get that because she thought that the angelic beings were angels, the voice the Voice of God, and the entire story was an affirmation of faith, not in science, but in the Lord. She left uplifted and inspired.

When they sat in the planetarium café afterwards for a glass of wine, again Karen's treat, she didn't have a chance to discuss the story's themes.

"Thank you so much for tonight, Karen."

"Did you like it?"

"So much. I was kind of confused about the computers though."

"Althea. Tricia…"

Althea did not miss the name cue.

"I've valued our friendship these past months."

"So have I. So do I."

"You're a great compadre on our Saturday adventures but, beyond that, I trust you not to be shocked at what I'm really feeling in this place, not to rat on me."

"Of course. And I trust you."

"I'm leaving tomorrow morning, Tricia. I've given this HOME thing a shot, but it's not for me. You know why – we've talked about it lots of times – the control, the secrets, the strange expectations I can't seem to decode. I'm a simple Episcopalian girl, and I just want to worship God and lead a good life."

"Ah. I can't say I'm surprised, just sad." Althea wanted to ask her what she had decided about the High Calling and the Revelation of the Master, but she didn't want to argue, so she grinned and said, "At least you won't have to get used to being called by another name at life vows."

"Right – I just got lucky that they agreed not to change my name. They probably figured me for a short-timer." Karen's eyes twinkled mischievously.

"Where will you go?"

"Home – Corpus Christi, best home on earth. I miss Texas so much – the friendly people, the weather, the Gulf, and most of all my family. I'll be home for Easter, Tricia. The High Mass is so beautiful, and then my family has a picnic at the beach. It seems the whole universe is rejoicing in the Resurrection."

"It sounds so wonderful I wonder why you ever left, Karen?"

"Mmm, I guess because I'd always known that world and I wanted to explore a little, have some time to think about the direction of my life. And I have – I've decided to go back to school next fall at the University of Texas, San Antonio, to get an M.S. in Deaf Education. It's what I've always wanted to do with my life, and this year has made me even more certain. I've already been accepted."

"How did you manage to apply without Father Edwin finding out?"

"Easy – in January I rented a Post Office box with my savings, and asked my dad to send me some money to keep it up and to apply."

"Wow, you are brave. And smart. A Master's degree. I'm so proud of you."

Karen looked Tricia Althea in the eyes and said, "You don't need to be unique to finish an education, you know. You just need to decide you'll do the work and not give up."

"That's probably easier to say when you have people who believe in you and get what your goals are – especially your mother and father."

Karen laughed. "That's quite an assumption, Tricia. My parents love me unconditionally, but neither of them finished college, and a B.S. was their big dream for me, not a Master's degree. They'd be perfectly happy if I took a job doing interpretation. I had to do some fancy talking to convince my dad to send the application money, and all on a payphone, but he finally agreed. I'm the one who believes in my career."

"I'll remember you said that."

They'd need to leave very soon to make curfew. Even while she had become somewhat critical of her inclination toward dramatic gestures, Tricia Althea removed her favorite pierced earrings – the silver half-moons which she had worn in honor of the planetarium show, spooned up a little red wine, and dropped the earrings into the spoon while Karen watched quizzically. After a moment, she lifted them, dried them with her napkin, and extended them to her friend.

"Remember me."

Karen's hand closed over the hand that extended the gift. "How could I forget you, my friend?"

CHAPTER TWELVE

A House Mother

March 1976 – Reverend Catherine

Halfway through their year of training was an odd time for Headquarters to send these students a House Mother, but Reverend Catherine understood that it couldn't be helped. Female priests were few, and most were needed at the big centers in San Francisco and St. Louis. Reverend Catherine herself had been ordained less than three months ago at Christmas, barely enough time to practice performing the services before being shipped out from San Francisco to Colorado. Of course, Reverend Michael, her fiancé, had been sent to New York which seemed a million miles away. They couldn't live at the same site as House Parents until they were married since that could invite rumors, and Reverend Catherine needed to become familiar with being a priest before she took on the role of a wife. This explanation of the White Brotherhood was all very logical and wise, but it didn't convince her lonely heart.

She was resolved to throw all her energies into serving these students. Even though Father Edwin gave her a detailed introduction just before dinner on the night she arrived, the first item on her agenda was to have each student Sister and Brother sign up for a one-on-one conference. They needed to know that she was approachable and that they could trust her. Sister Althea was one of the first to sign up. Reverend Catherine had heard about this student from Father Edwin as well as the Novice Master, Mother Ursula, but she would make up her own mind.

"Come on in," Reverend Catherine replied to the polite knock on her open office door. "You're Sister Althea," she said with her warmest smile.

Sister Althea smiled back, nodded, and took a seat.

"How are you doing today?"

"Uh, okay."

"How was work?"

"Work went pretty well today. I work as an aide at a nursing home; did you already know that? I try to get most of the chores done in the morning so I can have some time with the patients in the afternoon. There's this one patient named Edith who sits in the hall and cries or asks whoever's walking by whether her family is coming. They never do. The nurse, Angela, let me take her to her room today to listen to her talk about when she was a kid. Sometimes it's pretty disconnected and hard to follow, but today the story was great. She was a very little girl when her parents brought her to Creede, Colorado for the second silver boom. They missed the first one, she said, because she and her baby sister were too young, but the second boom brought them all the way from Indiana. It was so exciting. At first they lived in a tent, then in a wooden shed, but soon her father made a lot of money and moved them to a beautiful house in Denver. She was a part of history! Of course, she can't remember who I am from one hour to the next. Am I talking too much?"

"Not at all. That's quite a story, and it tells me a lot about you. You have a hard job but a good one, and you give your heart to it."

"Thank you. Vow of service, right?"

The rest of the meeting was uneventful. Sister Althea had been well. She didn't need anything that she could think of. She missed her friend, Karen. Obviously more was going on under the surface with this basically healthy girl who was carrying about twenty extra pounds on her petite frame. Stress? Anxiety? Trauma? Time and trust might help her to help.

ALTAR CALL?

April, 1976, Sister Althea

"A bunch of losers who can't figure out whether they're Presbyterian or Rosicrucian," Jana had called the HOME Brotherhood, and her acid tongue had burned into Althea's memory deeply enough that, when HOME's new project was launched, the words leapt to Althea's mind. This spring, Father Edwin explained, the Brotherhood was launching a return to the traditional Protestant revival. Though still trusting the High Calling and of course the Master, Althea had become skeptical enough of the human leadership of this group to wonder. What did revivals have to do with their basically Episcopalian or Catholic liturgy? With the New Age goals of Illumination and Self-Realization? With any revelation from the Master?

"This is a way for us to reach people who are not as spiritually adept as we are," Father Edwin explained. "It is a familiar door, which can lead many into the mysteries."

Really? Or was it a marketing strategy? Though Jana hadn't responded to letters and phone calls over the past months of student training, Althea had trusted her through some of most difficult periods of her life. Jana's voice could be harsh, but she was fiercely committed to telling the truth as she understood it, and right now Althea was having a hard time understanding on her own.

Over a number of weeks, Father Edwin taught them the history, how this movement had strengthened Americans' faith during the late 18th and early 19th centuries. He taught them the components of a tent revival – lots of hymns to stir the heart, a fiery sermon urging repentance, and an altar call. He was so drily academic about it that Althea wondered what he really thought of the project, but then he was also under obedience.

The Brotherhood actually had a large tent set up, in the grand tradition of The Second Great Awakening, and erected a make-shift wooden altar on which was only a large metal cross. Neither religious pictures nor sacramental vessels were in sight, since these would have offended many in the intended audience. Audience was an accurate word, since the gathered Brotherhood was not praying as they themselves prayed, but putting on an elaborate performance.

The first tent meeting was bigger than she had imagined. More than two hundred locals arrived to fill the tent almost to capacity. Two other priests, one from Kansas and one from Nebraska, were visiting for the week to help pull off the event, and of course Reverend Catherine assisted. Father Edwin officiated, even though the other, folksier clergy might have made a better initial impression. His wry, polished high church demeanor hardly fit the role. Did he see his audience – ranchers dressed in overalls or housedresses – or were the stage lights blinding him? Having studied public speaking, Althea knew that one of the key principles of public speaking was to know the audience and speak accordingly. But Althea stopped these thoughts, realizing how proud they sounded.

"Good evening, ladies and gentlemen. It is my honor to welcome you tonight to the first of this week's revival meetings. We hope tonight will inspire you to make or renew your commitment to the Lord. We will begin by singing some traditional hymns. Please join in; there's a paper hymnal on every seat."

The students had learned a number of historic hymns such as "Worthy the Lamb," "Babel's Streams," "Why Sleep We?" and "Wake, Isles of the South." Most of the them were repetitive, simplistic, and boring to Althea who had spent her first seventeen years, for both worse and better, in the Catholic Church – worse for the legalism and control and hypocrisy, but better, far better, for Masses by Bach, Hayden, Palestrina, Beethoven, and Mozart. Not only was that music exalted, but the theology was serious, even if she didn't completely agree with it now. Now the only hymn she responded to and sang in full voice was "I See You, Lord," which was directly from the Book of Isaiah:

I see you, Lord. I see you, Lord.
You are high and lifted up and your train fills the temple.
You are high and lifted up, Lord, and your train fills the temple.
And the angels cry "Glory," and the angels cry "Glory,"
and the angels cry "Glory" to Our God.

They must have sung for close to an hour. Soon the visitors were swaying back and forth or side to side and raising one or both hands in the air. Their faces were full of emotion; some wept, and others called out spontaneously, "Praise You, Lord! Praise Jesus! Amen!" Meanwhile Father Edwin stood to the side, watching quizzically the spectacle he had helped to create. Finally, he nodded to the student choir to signal the final song. It was time for the sermon.

Father Edwin took as his text a passage from St. Luke, Chapter 12: "I am come to send fire on the earth…. Suppose ye that I am come to give peace on earth? I tell you, Nay; but rather division…." Now the HOME House Father was in his element, harnessing his fiery nature to stir the listeners to repentance. They listened on the edge of their seats, in rapt attention, with the occasional outcry of enthusiasm. He concluded by shouting out verse 8: "Whosoever shall confess me before men, him shall the Son of man also confess before the angels of God…" and inviting all who were moved to come to the altar rail where he and the other priests would lay hands on them.

The student choir began singing again. A few people, then more and more, made their way to the altar. Althea couldn't focus on singing for wondering what that altar call was supposed to mean.

Later that night, she took a chance and confided to Reverend Catherine what she was feeling. If her House Mother told this to Father Edwin, Althea would be in trouble, but there was a good chance that kind and easy-going Reverend Catherine might not tell. There was something about this pretty blonde woman who sang in the hallways, always had a kind word, and was nearly as young as Althea.

Reverend Catherine searched Althea's eyes, and perhaps searched her own heart, before responding.

"You're very perceptive, Sister Althea, and I can't lie to you, but I'm under obedience not say too much. You're right that these revivals are window-dressing. They are not really our work. Our work, which is our own perfection, is spiritual and unseen. Just wait a while until you're Illumined and Self-Realized and you'll start to understand. Then you'll know the power that's in you, and you won't need all these outer forms."

"Thank you for being honest with me, even though I'm a student. I'm grateful that you're here", Althea answered.

But while she was relieved to have her sincere perception confirmed, she was deeply troubled by the rest of Reverend Catherine's response, which seemed to have more to do with personal attainment than with God. And what about all those trusting people?

That night before she fell asleep, Sister Althea closed her eyes to see the tiny flecks of light that HOME called "yods" after the letter from the Hebrew alphabet. These were not, of course, "The Light," because she had seen them since she was a little girl, but they were part of the deep, still night in which she believed with all her heart that God was with her, loving her, helping her in spite of her confusion because God is love. God is also truth, and she gave thanks that, emotional as she knew herself to be, she had not responded to the phony altar call.

CHAPTER FOURTEEN

THE WALKWAY TO THE CHAPEL ON AN AUGUST NIGHT

Sister Althea – August 1976

It was impossible to find a spot in the Student Center to be alone, but after evening prayers one night in August, Sister Althea stayed behind in the chapel until everyone had left, sat on the floor facing a back corner, and wept.

Next week the students would take their vows of celibacy and begin a year of focused prayer and service. The vow didn't faze her; she'd lived under the vow of purity for a year, and chastity was meant only to intensify the focus by postponing for a year any close friendships with anyone, either women or men. It was really the life of a nun, but just for a year, and that was what she had wanted when she was in high school, to live as a nun for a time and then get married.

No, what it came down to now was trust – she was losing trust in HOME but she had no idea who or what else to turn to. She wasn't about to return to the Catholic Church and all the protestant practices that she knew about were even more human-created and partial. One Christian, no Christian, she'd heard it said, meaning that we need community to keep us connected to God. Her own years of trying to live a decent life on her own were proof of that. How easily she'd become selfish, self-indulgent, confused.

And where would she even go to start over? Certainly not back to her family. Jana wasn't speaking to her. She had about ten dollars and a suitcase.

The more she considered all of this, the harder she cried, until she felt a gentle hand on her shoulder – Reverend Catherine.

"I thought everyone was gone," Althea said, turning herself to face her House Mother.

"I know. Everyone was gone, but I came back for a book. I cry sometimes here too, you know, because there's no privacy in the house. May I sit down?"

Althea nodded. Reverend Catherine took a cross-legged position across from her and waited.

"I don't know what to do," Sister Althea said finally.

"About what?"

"About my life."

"Oh, my, your whole life? What's the matter with your life?"

And now was a moment of decision. Reverend Catherine was a genuine person and she seemed honestly to care, but she was a priest in this order, which meant she had made many, many commitments, which meant she was sure of what she was doing, or at least thought she was. How could she hear Althea's doubts, fears, and reasons? Althea would have to keep this simple.

"I don't think I can stay, and I don't have anywhere to go." The tears returned, now fueled by frustration at not being able to explain why.

"Ah. Well, first of all, don't judge yourself. This is a huge commitment and everyone has doubts. What I try to remember is that the Master Jesus has called us to the High Calling. Do you believe that?"

"That's what I've been hanging onto for the last year and a half. I believe that Jesus has called me, but I don't know any more if it's to this."

"Okay. So that's part of what the next year is for. All your vows are temporary, and you have a chance to give yourself over to trying to fulfill them. If that doesn't work, it doesn't, and you'll be free to leave and go back to the world. Wouldn't you like to try though? To have a higher, greater life?"

"That's all I've ever wanted. Is that what's been happening for you?"

"Yes, Sister Althea, it is."

"Reverend Catherine, have you ever had doubts?"

"Of course. It's human to have doubts, but I've kept them to myself and persevered. I'm glad I did. I'm honored that I was made a priest, and in about a year I'm going to marry the most wonderful man. Life is very sweet. You've already come so far, Sister Althea. Don't you want to give the next year to the Master?"

Reverend Catherine actually seemed very happy, happier than any other people she'd known in HOME. Maybe she was right. Maybe someday she could be like Reverend Catherine – a normal, kind life-vowed Sister who didn't think she was better than the students, who talked to them like people, who told her the truth about her own heart, who freaking KNEW her own heart and not just what people told her she was supposed to be feeling. Maybe someday she would know who she herself was and what she was feeling and she would tell the truth about it, and finish school, and be able to teach and write. Then one of the brothers would fall in love with her and they would get married.

"I'll try," she said.

"Good for you. You're brave, Sister Althea." Reverend Catherine gave her a big hug and they went to the kitchen for a cup of tea.

The next day she said goodbye to Angela the nurse and gave her the precious cross pendant Jonathan had given her. That night she took the vow of celibacy, and at 6:20 the next morning she left for St. Louis on a Greyhound bus in the company of ten other Sisters.

PART FOUR

THE SISTERS OF MERCY

CHAPTER ONE

WELCOME TO THE MOTHERHOUSE

Sister Althea, September 2,1976

The cook, Sister Olivia, was a very tall, boney, no-nonsense person. She met the new sisters at the bus station, but she had little to say. It was Mother Esther, standing unsmiling at the top of the long and wide front staircase, who received her charges, as they lugged their suitcases up the mountain of stairs and introduced themselves one by one. Regardless of her short, plump physique, the Abbess radiated energy and authority. Maybe it was partly her red hair; maybe it was the fire in her eyes.

Sister Althea was exhausted. The trip itself had taken twenty-six hours, not to mention the wait to collect the luggage and the drive across town. Sister Sandra in Denver had provided each of them with a bag of sandwiches and bottles of water, so she wasn't starving hungry, but she had never been able to sleep in public and had been awake all night. The last thing she wanted was a ceremony, and yet that was what was expected.

Now the Abbess took her by both arms and said, "I am Mother Esther, your Abbess."

She had been listening as the sisters in front of her were coached in the proper response, so she answered, "Bless you, Mother Esther. I am Sister Althea, your student."

"Greetings, Sister Althea. Welcome to the Motherhouse."

That was it. She picked up her suitcase and entered. Sister Olivia led the Sisters to their shared rooms, instructing them that lunch would be served at noon but they were welcome to rest until dinner at six. As soon as the door closed, Sister Althea grabbed the towel from her bed, found an open bathroom before they were all taken, and washed off the travel grime. Then she lay down in her bathrobe and passed out.

She woke to Sister Olivia's knock.

"I have brought your everyday robes for you to wear to dinner tonight. You will receive dress robes later on. I will collect your black clerical dresses which you will not need this year."

The everyday robes were tan cotton with a generous hood, and they tied at the waist with a long, braided rope. Sister Olivia spread out an assortment of sizes on the one vacant bunk and the sisters sorted them until they each found one that fit.

Just before going to dinner, Sister Althea studied herself in the mirror. She looked serious in the new robe, unadorned, almost monastic. Almost.

CHAPTER TWO

UNTRIED AND UNAWARE

Mother Esther, September 2, 1975

This was Mother Esther's second year as Abbess of the Motherhouse. It was not to be a permanent assignment – she did want to marry eventually – but the gravity of the work here required experienced guidance. She was to maintain a strict rule of prayer and service, to counsel against any close relationships or self-indulgence, and to uphold the spiritual growth of the sisters as the first priority. In this way she was to serve these young women, not by giving way to their emotions and desires.

Growing up in a Conservative Jewish home, Esther had been well-trained in discipline and law. Her family kept the dietary laws and strictly observed the Sabbath. From her early years, she had learned Hebrew, and at twelve she had celebrated her Bat Mitzvah. For a decade more she did exactly what was expected of her, completing with honors a degree in Religious Studies. It was during that course of study that she began to question, to wonder. When she met a member of HOME on her college campus, she listened to him, and even attended some evening classes, but it was only after graduation that she seriously explored the teachings, joined, became a life-vowed sister, and eventually became a priest. For her, HOME had always been a path to God.

These students had such different stories from hers. Some had been hippies, some drug addicts, some just confused kids lost in a culture that was disintegrating around them. Where was their focus, their zeal? She would have to help them find it. They could not be here just because they had nowhere else to go. "For the zeal of Your house has consumed me, and the humiliations of those who blaspheme You have fallen upon me." This was one of her favorite verses from Psalms; she had often heard it read at Jewish funerals. Now it applied so well to her role that she had begun to recite it every morning.

In a Catholic convent, the word of the Abbess was law, and this renunciate sub-order was modelled after a Catholic convent. That night before dinner, Mother Esther stood before her new charges as their ultimate authority, the first and last word, to set a tone for the coming year.

"Sisters – again, welcome. You have passed the tests of your student year and are ready to take on greater challenges. Remember your High Calling. Remember that you have been chosen to help usher in a new age of enlightenment – but only if you prove yourselves worthy. How will you do this? You are already familiar with the five basic vows, and you will continue to strive to fulfill them. Additionally, you will pray more intensely and serve more diligently now, both day and night. You will have little time for yourselves, little time for each other. This is all as it is meant to be. I hope for you the dedication that will allow you to meet the rigors of this year."

As she looked around the table at those many young faces, Mother Esther saw obliviousness, anxiety, and occasionally eagerness. It could be a long year.

CHAPTER THREE

A SPECIAL SCHOOL

Sister Althea – September, 1976

To her surprise, Sister Althea found a job almost immediately as a Teacher Aide II in Booker T. Washington Special School in downtown Saint Louis. She was assigned to the junior class for Business English and Business Math.

When she walked into the classroom, chaos prevailed. The students were talking, laughing, eating, throwing things. One was leaning out the window smoking a joint. Others were obviously already high. She eventually found the teacher in a back room behind the classroom and introduced herself. She was an attractive black woman in her thirties, well-dressed but with an exhausted demeanor.

"Hi. I'm Janis. I'm glad they finally got me some help."

"I'm glad to help, but I'm confused. This hour is Business English, right? What are they doing?"

"Oh, Business English? That's a euphemism. These kids can't read or write, or else won't. They all got left behind somehow. Some of them have learning disabilities that I have no clue how to deal with because I am just a regular high school English teacher,

Lord help me. A few have recently been released from juvenile detention and they are mad as hornets. Two of the girls are returning to school after having a child. There is one with epilepsy so keep an eye out. He's the one who sits in the far left corner. He could have a seizure any time."

Sister Althea was silent for a moment before asking, "So, how can I help?"

"Your guess is as good as mine. Do whatever you like. I gave up on them a couple of years ago."

That night and every night for the next week, Sister Althea went home from work and cried. Any attempts at creating order in the class were met with indifference or even hostility. One girl pulled a knife and told her she'd like to kill her, and the others laughed. Althea asked Janis to get security but by the time the officer came the girl had disposed of the knife and denied ever having it. The class backed her up. Nothing was done.

Helping these kids was her service, though, so she kept praying and kept showing up. Eventually she would figure it out.

CHAPTER FOUR

STORIES

Charlene, a Senior at the Special School – November, 1976

This new white girl teacher was weird from day one, all "I want to help you" and stuff. What did she know about them, about their lives and what would help them? For one thing she – Charlene – needed a babysitter for her little girl, somebody besides her mama who was working nights so Charlene could finish high school during the day. Dang that Leroy, all "I love you, Charlie baby, I'd do anything for you." Sure. Where was Leroy now? Nowhere since their baby was born. Yes, the baby was his, had to be his. He was the only one, the only one ever. Dang him! Then this white girl maybe a couple years older than she was shows up and wants to help. Brings them greasy cookies and tries to teach them math. One day Charlene had about enough and told her she hated her. White girl doesn't even blink, just says okay but I like you and I'm here to help you graduate. There it was again – she was going to help – and before Charlene knew what she was doing she'd pulled her knife and flashed it in this girl's face and told her she'd like to kill her.

She didn't mean it, didn't want to hurt her. She had never even been in a fight, just carried a knife for protection on the street. She just wanted this girl to quit trying so hard and leave them alone like Ms. Janis did. She'd had it up to the eyeballs with people saying they wanted to help and not helping. Sooner or later they were going to get a diploma and leave anyway – the school couldn't keep them there forever because there were always new kids coming in and besides nobody cared much what happened to them, whether they could read or write or do math or ever got a real job. So what? Bring 'em in and move 'em through, that was what the school did. The uptight principal came by to ask about the knife but she'd already ditched it, she denied having it, and the whole class said the new teacher made it up. He left and nothing ever happened.

But this new girl didn't quit. This nerd in dumpy second-hand clothes with her hair all wound tight in a knot like an old lady, who'd have known she'd have the guts to stay? Only white girl in the building. She stayed, and one day she walked into class, sat down on the edge of the desk, and didn't say a word, just opened this book and started reading to herself. They all looked at each other. This was maybe the weirdest thing she'd done yet.

"Hey, what you reading?" somebody asked.

She acted like she didn't hear.

"Hey, teacher, what you reading?"

Slowly, she looked up. "I am reading a story," she said, and started reading again to herself.

By this time nobody was talking, just watching her. But Charlene liked stories. She was in a regular high school before she got pregnant and she read a lot before she had to leave school last year. Sometimes she'd read a story in the school library during study hall, and sometimes it'd be a good story about somebody real and all. Finally, she said, "So teacher, what's the story?"

"Oh," she said, looking up from the book acting all surprised that Charlene wanted to know. "It's called *Go Tell It on the Mountain* –"

"So it's about religion like you're all about religion, right 'Sister' Althea?" she drawled sarcastically.

"No, Charlene," she said, looking her in the eye, "it's about being young and wanting a good life and having to deal with racism and people acting hatefully and what a person can maybe do about it."

"Humph. What do you know about all that anyhow?" A couple kids behind Charlene laughed sarcastically.

"From experience, I don't know much about racism because I am white. You've probably noticed that. In the small town where I grew up most people looked pretty much like me, and I didn't think about that much, but I dated a young black man while I was going to high school in Buffalo. I know he was smart and ambitious but he went to a public high school that wasn't well-funded and he had to work hard to succeed. I know a little about how he felt when my friends didn't want to hang out with us even though his friends were kind to me and asked me to their parties, and even though he was president of Junior Businessmen and an honor student and I thought he was more accomplished and interesting than most of their boyfriends by far. You're right – I didn't feel his anger and insult, but I felt my own because it just wasn't right. That's not much to know, I guess, but I've read a lot. Like this book. I read it when I was in high school while I was dating Noah. And I read a lot of other books too because I was trying to understand better what his life was like."

Dead silence in the room. Even Charlene, and it took a bit to shut her up. That was the most this white girl had ever said all at once, and while she talked, her feelings came out in her words in a way that couldn't be faked. They all looked at each other. Maybe this girl was human after all.

"What happened to him? To Noah?" Charlene said finally.

"He went to a big university out of state on a full scholarship and I, well, let's just say life at home wasn't all it should have been when I was in high school and my grades weren't good, so I stayed in our small town and worked at the grocery store and went to a junior college. He met somebody else and that was that. I wish him a good life."

Dang. She was human. Charlene turned around to the others and gave them a thumbs up.

"Can you read us that story?" Charlene asked.

"Would you like that? What do all the rest of you say?"

They mumbled and nodded yes, and she started.

The story was about this boy, John, about their age, Charlene guessed, or maybe a little younger. You could tell he was black by the way he worshipped at church, and the way the family was, and then there was the part about the yellow stain on the ceiling and the sound of rats' feet and the cursing from the harlot's apartment downstairs – he lived in the projects for sure. Teacher said later that this place was Harlem in New York City, but it sure could have been St. Louis. His daddy beat him and his brother but come to find out it wasn't their real daddy, but their mama said he beat them because he loved them. Right. Heard that one before. But John was smart. Everybody told him that, same as everybody told Charlene that.

John went walking in places where black people didn't live and probably couldn't live because they wouldn't even let him go into a store in those hoods. And then teacher read words she would never forget and she would do something about if she could:

This world was not for him. If he refused to
believe, and wanted to break his neck trying,
then he could try until the sun refused to shine;
they would never let him enter. In John's mind,

then, the people and the avenue underwent a change,
and he feared them, and he knew that one day he
could hate them if God did not change his heart.

Teacher stopped reading right there, maybe to let it sink in, and it did. They all just stared at her and she closed her eyes for a minute before she started talking. Knowing her, she was probably praying.

"This story was published in 1952, the year I was born. It has the "N" word in it because people still got away with talking like that in 1952. Some very brave men and women have been fighting racism since then, Reverend Dr. Martin Luther King through non-violent civil rights marches, and the writer of this story, James Baldwin, through writing stories and making people more aware. It's taking a long time to make things right, but some people are trying to make things better.

"Should I read more tomorrow?"

Nodding heads, mumbles of "Yeah."

"All right. We'll start where we left off. Now let's talk about fractions."

Teacher read that book every day for a couple of months. The ending was no happily ever after, but it made Charlene feel strong and brave. Teacher told them about the writer, too, said he wrote more than twenty books and won awards and spoke at universities, and he could walk into any store he wanted to.

Maybe writing stories really was a way to make things better. Charlene figured maybe she could do that too.

CHAPTER FIVE

A GLIMPSE OF THE LIFE

Sister Althea — Winter, 1976

Sometimes it was the mundane, day to day things that seemed the most difficult. No matter how hard Sister Althea tried to settle into her situation, the crowding in the Mother House continued to shock her, and life continued to be hard – physically and emotionally hard.

Nearly fifty women lived in this Mother House. Granted, it was a stately, if ancient, house with beautiful and comfortable common rooms downstairs, but eight sisters slept in each of the small bedrooms, in HOME's ubiquitous bunk beds – and Sister Althea was enduring another year on the bottom bunk. The house had only four full baths, and one of these was usually reserved for the life-vowed women. With the Sisters' already challenging schedule, this meant that often she needed to get up at 4:30 am to take a shower before the bathrooms were taken. Either that, or she could wait until everyone finished showering at night after prayers ended at 10 pm.

That number of people inevitably made quite a mess, too. It was one of Sister Althea's duties to clean upstairs when she arrived home from work, and it was everyone's duty to help with dinner dishes before going out for their evening service.

Wakeup for the sisters was at 5 a.m., chapel at 5:15, breakfast at 6:00. Sister Althea had to leave for work at 6:30, so she was excused from breakfast dishes. She walked to the bus in the snow, waited in the wind, rode across the city to the projects, and reported to work by 7:30 a.m. That is, if the bus was on time, and sometimes it wasn't. If she arrived 5 minutes late she was written up by the principal, a stern man dedicated to running a tight ship administratively, which stood in stark contrast to the chaos reigning in every classroom. After a time, when by prayer, trial, and error she had managed to find a way to engage the students, she enjoyed teaching very much, and to her delight she was able to teach some of them to read and write a little.

The bus ride home at 3:30 pm was a little less crowded, so she usually arrived back to the house around 4 p.m., when she began her assigned chore of dusting and vacuuming the second floor. Sometimes she had a little time for stretching exercises before chapel at 5:30 pm and dinner at 6 pm.

On Tuesdays and Thursdays, though, she took a different bus straight from work to the nearby town of Clayton, where she volunteered as a counselor for the Suicide Prevention Service from 5 p.m. to 8 p.m. Like teaching at the special school, this work was demanding but extremely rewarding. Thankfully, the callers were usually much more interested in a sympathetic ear than in actually committing suicide, but counselors needed to be very alert and cautious all the same. Before the conversations got too far, they would ask whether the callers had a plan for taking their lives, whether they had arranged a way to take their lives. If the answer was yes, they would ask for an address and have an associate call 911. If the caller refused to provide an address, they would have an associate call 911 and try to keep the caller on the phone as long as possible so that the police could trace the call. Whether or not it was an emergency, sometimes she would listen for hours while people told their sad and lonely stories. A man's wife had died several months before and he could not get over his grief. A young, unmarried, pregnant woman had been thrown out of her angry parents' home and felt she was burdening the friends she was staying with. Sister Althea never gave advice, just listened – and prayed.

The bus usually got her home in time for chapel at 9 –10 p.m., then perhaps a shower, if one of the bathrooms was open, before collapsing into bed. Of course she missed dinner, but Sister Olivia, though she so seldom smiled or even spoke, always kindly remembered to leave her a plate of food on the stove, which she would devour after chapel. Once, during a storm, she arrived quite late for chapel, and simply sat down in the kitchen to eat dinner. Mother Esther came looking for her before she had taken more than a couple of bites.

"Sister Althea! What do you think you are doing?"

Sister Althea leapt to her feet. She hadn't felt guilty about eating – until this moment. "Mother Esther, my bus was very late and I knew that evening prayers were almost over, so I thought –"

The color rose to the Abbess's cheeks, highlighting her many red freckles. This was going to be bad.

"You thought? You THOUGHT? Who directed you to think about whether or not to attend chapel? You are under OBEDIENCE to attend chapel, no matter how late! Do you not realize that this is the highest spiritual training center on earth? Do you not know what a privilege it is for someone like you to be here, to be cleansed and made worthy? You are being prepared for a new age of enlightenment, to prepare others for a new age of enlightenment. Do you not know the great responsibility you have been given? Are you instead concerned with your stomach? Get upstairs to the chapel right now and meditate on this, and maybe you will learn something!"

"I'm sorry, Mother Esther," Sr. Althea whispered, as she covered her dinner and made her way to the chapel. What she did was so often not right, not enough, not spiritual enough, she thought as she mounted the two flights of stairs to the third floor chapel. Sometimes it was so hard to know what was spiritual or right; it kept changing, or what of it that was revealed to her kept changing, and she was expected to keep up with some mysterious set standards she wasn't aware of. She did not meditate in the chapel. She just talked to God and told Him her thoughts, and cried.

Weekends had their consolations. On Saturday evenings after dinner they had recreational time, and she was able to enjoy a glass of wine and a conversation with some of the other student Sisters. On Sundays after services, she liked to listen to a recording of Bach's *Brandenburg Concerti* which seemed well-suited to a Sunday afternoon in the stately parlor of the nineteenth century mansion they lived in. As the weather warmed in late spring, she took walks down Union Street. The Sisters would serve themselves a light supper of fruit and yoghurt before chapel. And the week would begin again. And again. And the year sped by in service and attempting to pray. But how much can really be said about that sincere attempt to pray? It is all inner and between oneself and God, and it is only He who can mark any progress.

CHAPTER SIX

TRIED AND FOUND WANTING

Sister Althea, St. Louis, April, 1976

Though it is God Who marks the progress of the soul, it is the Abbess who marks the progress of the student Sister, and during the final week of the renunciate year, each of these Sisters had a dread meeting with their Abbess, Mother Esther. One at a time Tricia saw her fellow students enter her office trembling and emerge smiling, congratulating one another on being accepted to take final vows. One afternoon, though, Sister Cecilia, who had spent the year teaching first grade at an inner city school and scrubbing bathrooms at the Mother House, was sobbing as she entered their shared room to pack.

Althea put an arm around her shoulder and waited for her to speak.

"I have to leave," Cecilia said finally. "I've done everything I could, and I have to leave."

"But why?" Althea said. "You've always been so obedient and cooperative – not asking questions all the time and making problems like I have. I've always thought you were a perfect Sister."

Cecelia smiled. "That's a sweet thing to say. I've tried my best, but I'm just not a good fit. I'm too simple, I guess. I don't understand the big ideas, not even enough to ask questions."

"It's not fair!"

"Life isn't fair, Sister Althea, but I believe that God is good, and He let this happen. I'm disappointed, but I accept it. There must be a reason I don't see."

"What will you do?"

"Oh, I'll go back to Indiana and keep teaching. I love the kids. I can stay with my family for a while; I've missed them. I just thought I could do something more with my life, but I had a good life before. It'll be okay."

The next morning, it was Sister Althea's turn. She entered the small office and sat facing the formidable Abbess.

"Tell me how you have fulfilled your vows, Sr. Althea."

"Yes, Mother Abbess. Poverty – I've held all things in common with the sisters, except for a few books and toiletries which I was willing to share. Purity – I've lived morally and worked to keep my thoughts pure. Obedience – I've followed the rules of HOME as far as possible and obeyed directives as I have understood them, even though sometimes I've failed. Service – I've taught high school in the inner city, given suicide prevention counseling, cleaned the Motherhouse, and helped prepare meals. Above all, I have tried at all times to serve God and obey His will for me. And the special vow of Chastity – I've tried my best to put God first in all things, even though I've sometimes failed in my heart and put other people and myself first."

Mother Esther nodded, and then was silent, apparently waiting. What was she waiting for?

"And?" she asked at last. "You've skipped one."

Althea recited the vows to herself in order. "Oh! Humility. I guess that's my worst one, isn't it? I mean, I've tried, Mother Abbess, but it's been hard to do things without understanding why, and sometimes it's been impossible to believe things without understanding them...."

"Yes, Sister Althea. This is one of our concerns about you. You have never really let go."

"What do you mean, 'let go', Mother Abbess? You've said this before, and so have others who advised me, but no one has been able to explain it."

Mother Esther looked at her hands for a moment, and then into Althea's eyes. "As you have meditated in chapel, Sister Althea, what have you seen?"

"Seen?" That question again.

"Yes. When you have closed your eyes and meditated, what have you seen?"

Over these two years and more, Althea had been repelling her own vivid imagination, praying that whatever spiritual experience she had would be genuine and God-given – God-given, and not given otherwise – not from her own fantasies, not from evil. But she had not been worthy of a true vision. That didn't surprise her. In her understanding, only truly holy people received true visions and she – well, she was only who she was, and of herself, how could she be anything else?

Before joining HOME, she'd always understood that it wasn't good to look for apparitions, much less to create them, that for most people they were of a dark, fallen nature, that it was best simply to pray and trust God to transform her. This was what she had always done in chapel. Although during countless hours she'd had a stream of images cross her consciousness, some more reverent than others, she could not honestly admit to having "seen" something, as in a vision or apparition. But that was what the Abbess was asking now, what had always been expected of her.

Now Mother Esther waited, searching her eyes penetratingly. "Sister Althea, what have you seen during meditation?"

"Just the things I've always seen when I've closed my eyes, ever since I was little. Particles of light. Negative images of things I looked at before I closed my eyes. No visions, Mother Abbess. God did not give visions."

"And you've had no profound experience of receiving the Light? Have you perceived a column of light rising up inside of you?"

"No, never. If I had, I would have been terrified."

"Ah. At least you are being honest, and not everyone is. You appear to be an ethical person, and you can be glad of that, Sister Althea – Patricia – may I call you Patricia?"

"My name is Tricia," she whispered under her breath. Mother Esther did not hear her, and didn't repeat herself. What good would it do to tell this person anything?

This was it – the cut. She admitted now that a part of her had always known it was coming. Still she was trembling uncontrollably, and then came the familiar experience she'd had since childhood, of being outside her own body, watching this thing happen as if to someone else – no vision, but a simple psychological escape she knew well. She breathed slowly, trying to calm herself.

"Patricia, life in HOME has not been a good fit for you, has it?"

How would she answer this? It had been hard, so hard, but she had come to believe it was her calling from God. She had said yes to that calling, again and again, every day. God does not abandon those who say yes.

She would not cry in front of this woman. She would not create a scene. If only she could stop shaking. She breathed slowly in and out, in and out. Lord help me.

"I never expected it to be easy. I've stayed because I believed I was called. Are you saying that's not true? What about the High Calling? What about becoming an Illumined, Self-realized being? Are you saying I'm not called to that?"

"That is not what I am saying, Patricia. You have another path ahead of you and perhaps in time you will become Illumined. Who is to know? I am saying that it is clear you are not called to be a life-vowed Sister in this Holy Order. This path demands surrender of self to the Way of Initiation, and full participation in our shared life without reservation. You have not approached that state, and for this reason you have not received Illumination with us."

And there it was. She did not belong. As she had not belonged in her family, or at school, or in a committed relationship with a man. As she had often not belonged in her own skin. Waves of fear washed over her, her heart pounded, and the room spun. Would she ever escape this recurring moment of wanting desperately to belong somewhere, to someone, to something – yet not belonging, not being able to accept things as they were given to her, not being someone who was accepted or, even when she was accepted, as her mother had accepted her, never believing she belonged.

If she responded to the Abbess again, she wasn't aware of it. Somehow she managed to rise and leave the room, to walk slowly to the garden, to stare at the pruned stubs of the rosebushes jutting out of the snow. Sister Lois's words in those first days of her novitiate returned to her:

"Ivy is for Faith. Hawthorne sprigs are for Hope. Roses are for Love. The three great virtues, Althea – Faith, Hope, and Love."

And then, an older and even deeper memory surfaced:

I said to my soul, be still, and wait without hope
For hope would be hope for the wrong thing; wait without
love
For love would be love of the wrong thing; there is yet faith
But the faith and the love and the hope are all in the waiting.

Not Scripture – which Scripture for this moment? – but poetry like Scripture.

CHAPTER SEVEN

GOOD FRUIT

Tricia, May 1977

The Abbess allowed Tricia to stay until the end of the school year, now keeping her earnings so that she had enough money to go somewhere else. Again. To begin again. Again.

Tricia was grateful for her teaching job. Not only did it get her out of the Mother House, away from silent looks of pity or judgement, but she had grown to love her work. Some of the kids had come far, writing and reading their own brief autobiographies, and others at least had let her affirm them by listening to their stories as she transcribed them and read them aloud. During the last two weeks, she typed all the stories, photocopied them, and stapled them into books they could keep, titled *Our Lives So Far.* The entire writing and reading project was one of the most worthwhile things she had ever done.

The special high school held a graduation dance and she was asked to proctor it. Sr. Kathleen, always kind and helpful, lent her a fancy, silky dress of an impossible mint green color, but still more appropriate than any outfit she could come up with from the shared closet. She felt a little like Cinderella escaping to the ball after the past two and a half years as a cinder maid with HOME, but with a fairy godmother who was colorblind.

The school lunchroom was decorated with balloons and streamers and Congratulations Graduate banners, and one of the grads was acting as DJ. Students were smiling, hugging each other, and most of all – dancing with all their hearts. The music was great, and Tricia stood in her proctor's corner moving her head and shoulders to the beat until, amazingly, Charlene approached her.

"Hey, teacher, here's my graduation picture. You can keep it and remember me."

"I will. Is this your daughter in the picture with you?"

"It sure is, that's Keena. She's three now, and she's a mess."

"She looks like you. Is she smart like you?"

Charlene laughed. "She better be. She's got to make it in this world."

"What's next for you, Charlene?"

Charlene's face lit up. "I got a job at a long term care facility, full time. It's as an aide, but it's at night so I can watch Keena during the day and my momma can work days and watch Keena at night while I go to school."

"You're going to school too?"

Her smile got even wider. "Yes, ma'am. I'm starting at St. Louis Community College next fall. I am going to be a teacher and write stories."

Tricia had no words, but threw her arms around Charlene before she could even think about it. Charlene, on this happy night, didn't object, but she did separate herself quickly.

"Hey, teacher, they're playing 'Billie Jean'! You want to dance?"

A little awkwardly, Tricia followed Charlene to the middle of the auditorium, began to move stiffly, and finally let go into the rhythm of the song. As she focused on the joy of Charlene's face, she moved more freely than she had in two and a half years.

When the music ended, Charlene grinned and said, "You dance like a white girl, teacher."

Tricia raised an eyebrow and grinned back. "I <u>am</u> a white girl, Charlene."

"Yeah, but you're okay."

ANOTHER ROAD

Late May, 1977

End of May. Most of the piled snow had melted, and here and there the green spikes of daffodil and tulip bulbs were pushing through the ground in the gardens on Union Street. Tricia's work at the special school was finished and she'd saved all that she was going to save – about three hundred dollars. It was time to leave, but where would she go? Certainly not backwards to where she had been, not to her parents' home or to Berkeley. Jana hadn't answered her letters. Timmy was newly married and deserved some space. She called Rita who was living in Santa Cruz.

"You're welcome here! In fact, you'd be helping me out. I lost one of my roommates last month. You'd have the nicest room in the apartment, the master, with a private bath. It's expensive, though. Do you think you could afford a hundred dollars a month?"

Tricia promised to pay the first month from her savings and look for a job right away. By now she knew how to keep looking until she found success. Bless Rita's big heart and love for her family. It would be so good to see her again. And Santa Cruz was right on the Pacific Ocean, the magnificent, powerful, regenerating ocean.

Early on the morning of May 22, 1977, Tricia prepared to leave the St. Louis Mother House for the Greyhound Bus station. She showered and dressed in a pair of jeans and a green sweater she'd purchased at a thrift store the week before, along with a small leather satchel. She didn't want to bring with her anything of her life with HOME, so she'd given her large blue suitcase to one of the Sisters who would need it for her life-vowed life. It took all of fifteen minutes to pack the new satchel with her now-tattered lingerie, a few toiletries, and the two precious books that had been with her so long: *The King James Bible* and *The Collected Works of T.S. Eliot.* It took less time than that to say goodbye to the people who had already gone on with their lives without her.

She was heading down Union Street toward the city bus that would take her to the Greyhound Station, smiling at the lightness of her load, when she heard someone behind her calling, "Althea, Althea!" It was Sister Olivia, running toward her at top speed, swinging her long legs and arms to catch up with her.

Unsmiling as ever, Sister Olivia reached out a large bag and said breathlessly, "You are going to need these sandwiches; the trip takes two days."

"This is so kind of you."

"It is nothing. Somebody has to tell you, though – you are going to have a good life." She grabbed Tricia's arms and looked fiercely into her eyes. "You are somebody that wants a good life, and you are going to have a good life. Do you understand?"

These were the most words Tricia had ever heard this person utter, and she wondered at the emotion that charged them. She wasn't quite sure she understood why Sister Olivia needed to tell her this, but she took the cook by the shoulders and said, "Thank you, Olivia. Is your name really Olivia? I mean, has it always been?"

The cook shook her head. "No. My name is Anne."

"Anne, please call me Tricia. My name is Tricia."